T0285997

MICKEY AND THE TEAMSTERS

UNIVERSITY PRESS OF FLORIDA

Florida A&M University, Tallahassee
Florida Atlantic University, Boca Raton
Florida Gulf Coast University, Ft. Myers
Florida International University, Miami
Florida State University, Tallahassee
New College of Florida, Sarasota
University of Central Florida, Orlando
University of Florida, Gainesville
University of North Florida, Jacksonville
University of South Florida, Tampa
University of West Florida, Pensacola

Mickey and the Teamsters

A Fight for Fair Unions at Disney

Mike Schneider

UNIVERSITY PRESS OF FLORIDA

Gainesville/Tallahassee/Tampa/Boca Raton
Pensacola/Orlando/Miami/Jacksonville/Ft. Myers/Sarasota

28 27 26 25 24 23   6 5 4 3 2 1

Library of Congress Cataloging-in-Publication Data
Names: Schneider, Mike (Michael Sidney), 1971– author.
Title: Mickey and the Teamsters : a fight for fair unions at Disney / Mike
    Schneider.
Other titles: Fight for fair unions at Disney
Description: 1. | Gainesville : University Press of Florida, [2023] |
    Includes bibliographical references and index.
Identifiers: LCCN 2023010658 (print) | LCCN 2023010659 (ebook) | ISBN
    9780813080307 (paperback) | ISBN 9780813073019 (ebook)
Subjects: LCSH: International Brotherhood of Teamsters, Chauffeurs,
    Warehousemen, and Helpers of America—Corrupt
    practices—Florida—Orlando—History. | Walt Disney Productions. |
    Teamsters—Labor unions—Florida—Orlando—History. | Disney characters.
    | Labor unions—Florida—Orlando. | Labor union
    locals—Florida—Orlando. | Amusement parks—Florida—Walt Disney World.
    | Walt Disney World (Fla.) | BISAC: HISTORY / United States / State &
    Local / South (AL, AR, FL, GA, KY, LA, MS, NC, SC, TN, VA, WV) | SOCIAL
    SCIENCE / Activism & Social Justice
Classification: LCC HD6515.T3 S36 2023 (print) | LCC HD6515.T3 (ebook) |
    DDC 331.87/20975924—dc23/eng/20230620
LC record available at https://lccn.loc.gov/2023010658
LC ebook record available at https://lccn.loc.gov/2023010659

The University Press of Florida is the scholarly publishing agency for the State University System of Florida, comprising Florida A&M University, Florida Atlantic University, Florida Gulf Coast University, Florida International University, Florida State University, New College of Florida, University of Central Florida, University of Florida, University of North Florida, University of South Florida, and University of West Florida.

University Press of Florida
2046 NE Waldo Road
Suite 2100
Gainesville, FL 32609
http://upress.ufl.edu

To Harvey and Leanne, also known as Mom and Dad; my partner, Erdem; and all the *mishpucha* . . . you know who you are

Contents

Cast of Characters

(In alphabetical order by last name)

Ed Chambers — Former head of the Service Trades Council Union.

Donnita Coleman-DuBell — A union steward for the costumed characters at Walt Disney World who helped push for changes at Local 385.

John "Spike" Coskey — A former official for Local 385 who was fired from the local and went to work for an outfit that tries to keep unions out of workforces. He has a son with Donna-Lynne Dalton.

Carl Crosslin — A Local 385 official who organized the costumed characters in the early 1980s.

Donna-Lynne Dalton — The longtime Teamsters business representative for the costumed characters at Walt Disney World who led a fight for union democracy against the president of Local 385.

Rom Dulskis — A top-ranking official at Teamsters Local 385 who was allied with Clay Jeffries.

Mario Ferenac — President of Local 385 in the 1990s.

James Hoffa — General president of the International Brotherhood of Teamsters from the late 1990s to the early 2020s and son of legendary Teamsters leader Jimmy Hoffa.

Walt Howard — A top-ranking official at Teamsters Local 385 who was allied with Clay Jeffries.

Clay Jeffries — The president of Local 385 whose controversial tenure was challenged by members who thought union democracy was disappearing under his leadership.

Sean Mason — A UPS driver who pushed for new leadership at Local 385 and ran on an insurgent slate of candidates.

Mike McElmury — Longtime Teamsters official in Florida who became trustee of Local 385.

Phillip Newell — A veteran worker in the costumed character department who helped push for changes at Local 385.

Larry Parker — President of Local 385 in the 1980s and early 1990s and son of Paul Parker.

Paul Parker — The first president of Local 385 when it was chartered in the late 1960s.

Ralph Singer — A driver in the movie industry who pushed for new leadership in Local 385 and ran on an insurgent slate of candidates.

Mike Stapleton — President of Local 385 in the 2000s and early 2010s.

Introduction

I've been a union member ever since I started working as a journalist for the Associated Press almost three decades ago. My union has fought on my behalf for health insurance, guaranteed wage increases, vacations, and a system of due process that has prevented the company from punishing me arbitrarily. More than anything, it has given me a sense of security against the whims of any mean-spirited managers or cost-cutting measures enacted by the company during tough economic times. I view my union as a comforting presence that will protect me, guide me, and offer me a community of colleagues who have my back.

Not every worker has those protections. At the start of the 2020s, less than one out of eight workers in the United States were represented by unions, according to the Bureau of Labor Statistics, and that figure was even smaller when it came to the percentage of actual dues-paying members, just over one in ten. That figure has dropped precipitously since 1983, when one in five workers were union members.[1]

Unions do a tremendous amount of good. Their decline in the past fifty years, often due to deliberate efforts to weaken them by businesses and politicians, is responsible for a lot of the disenfranchisement and alienation felt by working Americans nowadays.

But what happens when a union becomes undemocratic, turns on its members, and becomes the enemy? What happens when union leaders meant to look after their members retaliate against them, make them feel uncomfortable in the union hall, and refuse to represent them against the company they work for? That is what happened in the late-2010s to members of an International Brotherhood of Teamsters local in Orlando, Florida, and it wasn't just any group of workers whose union leaders retaliated against them. It was the costumed character performers at Walt Disney World in Florida, the ones who put the magic in the Magic Kingdom.

In a democratic union, members view themselves as part of an active culture of debate, participation, healthy elections, and a leadership that welcomes dissent. Leaders support an educated and active membership. University of Illinois labor scholar Steven Ashby has outlined a series of principles that define union democracy in his essay, "Union Democracy in Today's Labor Movement." There is financial transparency in the union local, and leaders are responsive to their members' concerns. The salaries of union leaders aren't that much higher than those of their members, and there regularly are contested elections.[2]

These principles of union democracy were lacking woefully at the Teamsters local in Orlando in the late 2010s. Instead, leaders earned several times what their members earned and had the perks of paid-for rental cars and annual Las Vegas trips. Children of the local's leaders were hired for jobs and became known as "children of the regime." Dissent was quashed and individuals who raised questions about the local's practices were targeted for punishment.

This book examines the consequences of troubled union democracy through the prism of what happened to the union that represents Mickey Mouse, Goofy, Cinderella, and other workers at Disney World. A good argument can be made that when union democracy is at its lowest—when the most important goals of union leaders are keeping jobs and making sure union dues keep flowing in instead of responding to members' concerns—unions are most vulnerable to attacks, weakened involvement by members, and declining membership. And that too happened to Local 385. Though the very rare union corruption often gets attention in the media, it is the lack of democracy that can have the most corrosive effects on American Labor.

The Teamsters and the Disney World costumed character performers made an unusual partnership, and I describe in chapter 1 how that marriage came to be. Bridging these two worlds was Donna-Lynne Dalton, a former Disney character performer who became a Teamsters leader for the costumed character actors. In chapters 2 and 3, I chronicle how Donna-Lynne came into this role.

I can't remember a time when I didn't know Donna-Lynne during my quarter century in Orlando, the nation's theme park hub. She always stuck out among the middle-aged, usually white, union men—they were primarily men—who represented the workers at Walt Disney World. Nowhere did she stick out more in her job than at the union hall of the Teamster local, whose troubled backstory as well as the rocky history of the International Brotherhood of Teamsters are examined in chapters 4 and 5.

In chapter 6, I demonstrate the importance of union work in protecting the performers who played costumed characters at Walt Disney World, particularly the advocacy carried out by Donna-Lynne. Chapter 7 delves into the history of unions at Disney World, and chapter 8 describes the fight over some of the most important contract negotiations in recent decades.

Being responsive to members' concerns is crucial for unions.[3] Without such responsiveness, unions are vulnerable to attacks, and that is what happened at the union for the costumed character performers, which I describe in chapter 9. Chapter 10 delves into the effort to bring back democracy to the Teamsters union representing Disney World workers through the efforts of a slate of reformers running to take over its leadership, and chapter 11 recounts the even greater undemocratic steps that Local 385's leaders took against the union's reformers in retaliation for their efforts to change what was happening.

In chapter 12, the costumed character performers lead the charge in revolting against the undemocratic actions of their leaders, and chapters 13 and 14 reflect on transitions that were going on with the Disney workers and Donna-Lynne. Chapters 15, 16, and 17 address the reckoning and subsequent fallout of Local 385's leaders.

This is a Disney story as well as a union story. So, it seems fitting to frame it as a fairy tale, with tongue stuck firmly in cheek.

. . . Once upon a time, in a far-off peninsula, an emperor of entertainment set up a kingdom of fantasy in the scrublands of central Florida. His name was Walt Disney, and his kingdom of princes and princesses, mice and men, was christened Walt Disney World. To keep this kingdom the size of the city of San Francisco running, Disney's business, the all-powerful Walt Disney Co., relied on an army of tens of thousands of employees who had come from around the globe to work in a world grounded in their childhood fantasies. Of all the workers of the kingdom, none were as exalted as the costumed character performers who played Mickey Mouse, Goofy, and Cinderella. They danced, signed autographs, led parades, entertained visitors, and helped the Disney kingdom generate billions of dollars in revenue, at least before the start of the coronavirus plague in 2020.

But life wasn't always magical for the character performers. It could get dangerously hot in their costumes during the brutal Florida summers. Children kicked their shins or tried to hang from their costumed noses. Managers sometimes punished them unfairly or fired them without reason. But the character performers had a fairy godmother protecting them. Her name was Donna-Lynne Dalton, and she worked as a business agent for the local affiliate of the International Brotherhood of Teamsters in Orlando. Rather than using a magic wand to turn pumpkins into coaches or tattered work clothes into ball gowns, Donna-Lynne used her negotiating skills to get better working conditions for her performers. She filed grievances against unjust treatment and made sure the terms of the performers' contracts weren't violated. Unlike the fairy godmother of Cinderella vintage, Donna-Lynne was neither plump, gray-haired, nor shrouded in a hooded gown. Rather, Donna-Lynne was a svelte former dancer who wore her hair in a girlish twist bun well into her fifties and looked about twenty years younger than her actual age. There was no "bibbidi-bobbidi-booing" from Donna-Lynne. She was a straight-talking former Philadelphian whose raspy voice betrayed a watchful, quiet toughness.

If the character performers were the Cinderellas of this story—working hard, early and late, to keep the Magic Kingdom running—then the Walt Disney Co. was Prince Charming, the princeling whose wealth was among the greatest in the land and whose partnership was desired by all. Rather than diamond necklaces and ruby rings, from their "prince" the performers at Disney World wanted job security, health-care benefits, and a pension that hopefully would carry them through retirement. Like Cinderella and the prince's nuptial agreement, the performers and the company had a contract that spelled out the terms and conditions of their partnership. The performers' hopes for a better life through the magical powers of collective bargaining and a structured system for pushing back against unfair company mandates was like the glass slipper that the prince puts on Cinderella. It fit due to the intervention of the fairy godmother, or in our real-world story, Donna-Lynne and the Teamsters.

But there wouldn't be a fairy tale without a disagreeable stepparent. In our labor tale, that stepparent was Clay Jeffries, the president of the local Teamsters affiliate, whose tenure was marked by efforts to punish Donna-Lynne and her costumed character performers, investigations, and a turn away from the principles of union democracy. Just as Cinderella's stepmother and stepsisters dictated the terms of Cinderella's happiness, so too did Clay and his associates create an environment for the character performers that became toxic and untenable. Clay and his henchmen began turning against the character performers in the late 2010s, and like Cinderella's stepmother, Lady Tremaine, they had an unjustified rage against the performers that threatened to turn the character actors' coaches back into pumpkins and Local 385 away from union democracy. The costumed character performers pushed back against the undemocratic, top-down management of their union in an effort to reclaim its mission of protecting and serving its members.

This is their story, told in several tales.

1

The Marriage

To begin with, it was a really strange marriage.

The tale of how Disney World's costumed character performers, who represent innocence and childhood fantasies, came to be Teamsters, a union known for truck drivers and past Mafia ties, started in the early 1980s, with the original matchmaker—a union organizer named Carl Crosslin.

It was 1982 and not long after former president Ronald Reagan had fired air traffic controllers in a watershed moment for the weakening of US labor unions. At the time, there was just a single theme park at Disney World, Magic Kingdom, built on central Florida scrub land that Disney had secretly acquired, parcels at a time, more than a decade earlier. The resort's second theme park, Epcot, would open just a few months later, and over the following decades, a third and a fourth theme park were added—what's now called Disney's Hollywood Studios and Animal Kingdom.

Crosslin, a Teamster business agent with a Tennessee drawl and an unloaded gun sometimes packed into his waist, had represented truck drivers at Disney World since before the theme park opened in 1971, when the truckers hauled construction equipment for the building of Magic Kingdom. At one point, he also was president of Local 385.

One day, while Crosslin was in a break room in the warren of underground tunnels hidden underneath Magic Kingdom, some character performers approached him. They knew he was a Teamsters business agent, and they asked him if he would help the costumed character performers join his union. Crosslin was intrigued. Here were performers who were the most visible workers at the theme park resort, and they wanted to join the union of Jimmy Hoffa, whose disappearance in the 1970s was one of the great mysteries of late-twentieth-century America. Though best known as a union for truckers and drivers, the Teamsters represented all kinds of workers, so Crosslin thought representing the performers behind Mickey

Mouse, Donald Duck, and Goofy might be a stretch but not completely out of the question.[1]

From his dealings representing workers in operations, maintenance, and transportation, Crosslin worked closely across the table with Disney World's vice president for labor relations. Disney officials respected him enough that they once had offered him a job to switch sides and join the company's labor relations team, but he turned them down. The Disney vice president told him to keep the organizing efforts of the costumed character performers low-key because, he said, "we don't want this stuff in the paper and everybody knowing what's going on." Crosslin was fine with that, but he warned the Disney vice president not to use a popular tactic for stopping organizing efforts then: hiring a good-looking guy, usually an actor, to sweet-talk the character performers, many of whom were women and gay men, out of joining a union.

"I know what you're going to try to do," Crosslin recalled telling the Disney executive. "You're going to do what Hearst used to do and get a good-looking guy out here and talk up all the girls, telling them, 'Oh, you don't want to go union.'"[2] Hearst, of course, was William Randolph Hearst, the newspaper baron. Although his newspapers favored progressive causes, Hearst was notorious for breaking strikes at his own newspapers in the early half of the twentieth century.

The Disney bigwigs in California ended up sending a Rock Hudson look-alike to Florida. He was six-foot-two and carried himself like the movie star. Crosslin spotted the Rock Hudson look-alike talking to the costumed character performers in the Magic Kingdom tunnels before and after shows, telling them that the company would take care of them. Crosslin was angry and vowed to throw everything he had into organizing the costumed character performers.

"I told [the Disney vice president], 'We will have a private vote, but once you start pulling that stuff, I'm coming after you,'" Crosslin recalled. "And he pulled it."

Crosslin came to the Teamsters by way of the machinists' union. He had arrived at the Teamsters to negotiate contracts for truckers and UPS drivers from Tallahassee to the Florida Keys, running up 85,000 miles a year on his truck without leaving Florida.

Crosslin started his drive to unionize the characters by talking to the performers individually to find out what they wanted. Their biggest concern was not more money but clean costumes and eliminating pubic lice from what they wore. "One guy told me the costume was so smelly he didn't want to put it on, but he did it because he needed a job," Crosslin said. The Teamster organizer promised the man that he would never wear a dirty costume again if he voted for the union. After that, Crosslin tried to smell as many of the performers' costumes as possible, so he could get a sense of what they were dealing with. "They all smelled pretty bad," he said.

The performers who played the smallest characters, like Mickey Mouse or one of the Seven Dwarfs, tended to be young women or little people. Even though the performers took great pride in bringing these animated characters to life, managers looked down on the costumed character performers and did not treat them with respect.

"Managers thought they were kind of stupid," Crosslin said. "You had midgets and you had dwarves. One dwarf said to me, 'I've never had another job.' After he said that, he told me, 'Don't look so sad.' And I said, 'I will because what else will you do if not this job?'"

The workers did not have enough time to get into their costumes in the tunnels at the start of their shifts. "They would say, 'Here's the costume. Get out there,'" Crosslin said. "They were filthy, and they would say, 'Go ahead and put them on anyway.'"

Crosslin's efforts were not the first attempt at unionizing the costumed character performers, who were categorized separately from performers who sang or acted with spoken lines at the parks. Those performers with singing or speaking lines were represented by the Actors' Equity Association, which wouldn't organize the singers, dancers, and actors at the parks until about a decade after the Teamsters' drive.

In the early 1970s, the International Alliance of Theatrical Stage Employees and Moving Picture Machine Operators had made a bid at turning the costumed character performers into a union bargaining unit, but federal labor judges rejected the idea in a slap to the characters' furry faces.[3] At the time, the sixty-two costumed character performers were called "pageant hosts and hostesses," and their job description, only two years after Magic Kingdom opened in 1971, included "being seen in the park, posing for pictures, participating in shows, and sometimes going on trips and appearing with other employees in television commercials." They were earning between $2.75 and $4.35 an hour.

Disney World officials argued that the costumed character performers did not deserve to be considered part of the theatrical workers' bargaining unit since they were no different from regular workers. They said all workers at the park were entertainers, not just the ones who dressed up as Mickey and Minnie. The company also argued that all employees wore costumes, not just the character performers, whether it was the "Jetsons"-like clothing for workers in Tomorrowland or the straw and felt hats in Frontierland.[4]

In late 1974, the matter went to a three-judge panel of the National Labor Relations Board, a federal panel that enforces labor law by investigating and ruling on claims of wrongdoing brought by workers, unions, or employers. The judges on the board said the costumed character performers did not belong in the bargaining unit with the theatrical workers, since they were no different than other Disney workers who operated rides or cleaned the park. The costumed character performers, they reasoned, worked the same hours, used the same entrances, shared the same break rooms, and worked side by side with other Disney workers. "The 'characters' are not actors; they do not constitute a craft," the National Labor Relations Board judges wrote. "They are essentially unskilled or at best semiskilled individuals whose working conditions, benefits, etc. are similar to those of other employees working in the Walt Disney World complex. In view of the foregoing, we find that the pageant host and hostesses do not have a community of interest separate from that of other employees to justify establishing them as a separate appropriate unit for bargaining purposes."[5]

That lack of respect for what the characters did, as shown by the judges, also carried over to Disney World management, according to Crosslin. Managers didn't provide the character performers with enough attendants to run interference for them against annoying guests, some of whom who would touch them inappropriately or punch the performers who dressed as Disney villains. A worker who played Captain Hook, Peter Pan's nemesis, told Crosslin, "If you can promise me that I won't be kicked in the shins by another kid I'll vote 'yes' for the union."[6]

"I said, 'You got it, buddy!'" Crosslin recalled.

Because Crosslin was already representing other Disney World workers, his badge gave him access to the all-important tunnels under the Magic Kingdom park where workers hung out. If he saw costumed performers in the tunnels, he would stop and talk to them. He staked out break rooms and bought coffee for performers in the cafeteria, meanwhile talking up the importance of being in a union. He got the weekly schedules of the shows being performed in the Magic Kingdom so he could catch performers before they went out into the public parts of the park and when they came back.

The character performers were unhappy with the favoritism shown by some managers and the lack of seniority in the handing out of assignments. They also did not like having a two-year limit on how long they could work as costumed characters and having to undergo periodic auditions to keep their jobs.

Before the character performers took their vote on a sweaty summer day in August 1982, almost a year after the drive began, Crosslin gave them his final pitch in the break room in the tunnels. "You want to be union? You are union. I'm just your mouthpiece," Crosslin said. He then grabbed a handful of plastic straws, first bending a single straw and then unsuccessfully trying to bend a handful of straws.[7]

"When they're all together, they're hard to break, right?" Crosslin recalled telling them. "The company tells you, now, what to do and not do. Well, we will tell the company what to do and not do."

The vote was a close 45 to 41 in favor of the costumed character performers joining the Teamsters.[8] But even then, some of the character performers doubted the Teamsters were a good fit for the workers who played lovable animated characters. "I don't see how that kind of union will help us," a performer who played Br'er Rabbit told the *Orlando Sentinel* after the vote. "It should be a theatrical unit of some kind." Other characters voted against joining the union because they liked a new manager who had once been a costumed character at Disneyland in California.

The character performers would not get a new contract until the following April as both sides haggled over terms. With the union contract, the characters got shin guards under their costumes to minimize children's kicks as well as more attendants with radios at their fingertips to keep away handsy people. The shift out in the park in the hot Florida sun was cut down to between twenty minutes and half an hour, depending on the temperature.

Even once the contract was approved and Crosslin was appointed to be the business representative for the costumed character performers, managers would try to make his life difficult, telling him that he could not visit certain places at the theme park resort, even though he was checking out the safety conditions for his workers. When that happened, he relied on his Teamsters temperament. "You go out there and try to be nice," Crosslin said, "but then sometimes you have to turn into a construction worker, and you got to cuss really loud."[9]

2

Little Snow White

The character performers would be represented by former truckers and machinists for the next two decades, until Donna-Lynne Dalton came to represent them in 1999. Unlike the burly former truck drivers and machinists who preceded her, Donna-Lynne was a pretty, petite former dancer and beauty pageant contestant. Donna-Lynne's diminutive size belied a toughness and low-boil intensity. She was the first Teamster representative for the character performers who had been one of them. She never forgot what it was like, especially how some guests would grope the performers in their costumes. "Some of them just want to see if you are a boy or a girl," said Donna-Lynne, stage-whispering, pretending to be a guest after finding out. "'It's a girl!'" "When you see those hands coming at you, it's time to run quickly," she said.[1]

Donna-Lynne was destined to be a union leader at Disney World. As a preschooler back in northeast Philadelphia in the 1960s, one of her first jobs was playing "Little Snow White" for a local television program. It was a union shop. Performing was in Donna-Lynne's genes. Her mother, Barbara, was a teacher of modeling and baton twirling, and Donna-Lynne insisted on being taken to Barbara's classes when she was a little girl. Her father, John, was a supervisor in the recreation department for the city of Philadelphia. Barbara and John met while working at the city's recreational facilities. John was a generation older than Barbara—he was fifty-four and she was twenty-three when they married—and they moved to the Burholme neighborhood of northeast Philadelphia. Donna-Lynne arrived three years later, in 1964. In yet another sign of her almost-preordained future with Disney, her mother nearly named her Bambi before the idea was nixed by her father. Donna-Lynne's name was a compromise, in tribute to a relative in California. Five years after Donna-Lynne arrived, her baby brother, Jack, who Donna-Lynne adored, was born. "I loved baby dolls. I loved Barbies. And now I had a real baby doll," she said.[2]

Donna-Lynne grew up in a union household. Her mother was a long-time member of the American Federation of States, County and Municipal Employees and was one of the few women working as a manager for the city's Department of Recreations at that time. Their neighborhood had been home to the country residences of Philadelphia's moneyed elite in the nineteenth century, but by the mid-twentieth century, it was solidly middle class. They lived in a "twin" home where two houses shared a wall.

As a child and teen in the 1960s and 1970s, Donna-Lynne performed in the thriving world of local Philadelphia variety and children's television shows. *The Wonderful World of Gene London,* Gene London's *Cartoon Corners, Al Alberts Showcase, The Chief Halftown Show,* and *Captain Noah and His Magical Ark* all filmed simultaneously in Philadelphia TV studios. In grade school, Donna-Lynne made weekly appearances on the Al Alberts Showcase, where little girls in party dresses would tell puns and dance and sing for the tuxedoed, graying-pompadoured crooner turned TV personality. Donna-Lynne regularly appeared on Captain Noah's puppet-heavy show and on the headdress-wearing Chief Halftown's cartoon show. She twirled batons on the celebrity-focused talk show *The Mike Douglas Show,* which was filmed for many years in Philadelphia before it moved to Los Angeles.

Donna-Lynne had gotten her first job on Gene London's show while her mother was working as a casting assistant on the program. London saw Donna-Lynne, who often came with her mother to work, and he wanted her as a pint-sized Snow White. Barbara resisted at first, since Donna-Lynne did not talk much at that age and Barbara worried that she would not be able to say her lines. But London persisted and Donna-Lynne did it. Donna-Lynne discovered that she loved performing—the dressing up, the sets, and all the artifice that went into constructing such wonderment. She got into trouble for wandering around the studio unsupervised and walking onto other sets, sending everyone into a tizzy.

By that age, as a preschooler, Donna-Lynne was entering toddler beauty pageants. She started with a win at the Little Miss Spray Pool title at a Philadelphia recreation center, and then she graduated to victories with the Little Miss Pennsylvania title in grade school and competition at the Miss Teen Globe, in which she competed at Walt Disney World, her first time at her eventual employer. She performed in children's roles at regional dinner theater productions of "South Pacific" and "Gypsy." When she was not performing on local television, she was taking endless lessons. From her mother, she learned baton twirling, acrobatics, how to model, and puppetry. Though Barbara gave Donna-Lynne her performer's spark, she was busy teaching her own classes. Students came from all over Philadelphia to learn baton twirling, modeling, and acrobatics from her, and Barbara often could not make it to Donna-Lynne's performances. As one of the few female managers in the city recreation department, she was very independent, and Donna-Lynne learned through her mother that a woman should always support herself. Her father, considerably older, had retired by the time Donna-Lynne was in fourth grade.

Donna-Lynne remembers one time sitting around the dinner table with her father and brother, talking about what she wanted to do when she grew up. She said she just wanted to dance for a living and have a son and a daughter of her own. Her father asked her if getting married was a good idea before she had children. She told him, "Nope."

Donna-Lynne learned to sing and dance from two women named Rita. She took singing lessons from Rita Cavell, who ran a well-known vocal studio in Philadelphia. Her dancing home was at the studio run by the Rita Ruh, who taught generations of Philadelphia performers, many of whom went on to successful show business careers.

Donna-Lynne's days were busy. After school, she would go to the taping of a show, or take a lesson, or make a promotional appearance with her dance-line group or match in Philadelphia's countless parades. Tuesdays and Thursdays, after school, were for drama classes. Saturdays were reserved for baton lessons. Dancing was her true love, and she did not mind missing episodes of "The Brady Bunch" to take dance lessons on Friday nights. She was always performing, and while she loved that, she enjoyed the rehearsal process even more. She liked learning new dance routines with her fellow dance-line hoofers and then, afterward, hanging out at the Broad Street Diner or the Melrose Diner, where the waitresses knew she had to have milk with her cake each night. Even though they were young teens walking into twenty-four-hour diners at midnight, nobody batted an eye. It was the 1970s, an era of laissez-faire parenting, and she would take the subway home and get up the next morning for school.

In eighth grade, Donna-Lynne entered a private prep school in northeast Philadelphia, even though she was baptized Catholic and regularly went to synagogue with her Jewish best friend. By then, she was being given responsibilities—both at work and at school—way beyond her years. She had graduated to a TV assistant job, as a fourteen-year-old, on the Al Alberts television show, and she would end up graduating from high school the next year at the age of fifteen. She did it by compressing the work of multiple grades into half the time. "I just did the assignments," she said.

"When there was an assignment, I just did the next one." It was awkward being several years younger than most of her peers, and though she got along with her classmates, if they remembered her at all, it was as "the little girl." She excelled in school, but her mind was always focused on dancing and performing. As her mother said, "She did well at school, but she didn't put in any overtime."

The TV studios were always buzzing with activity, and it was here that Donna-Lynne first took a role in leading performers. On Thursday nights, for *Al Alberts Showcase* at the WPVI-TV studios, Donna-Lynne led the group of young child performers known as the "Teeny Boppers" in rehearsing their jokes and helped them apply their makeup and get dressed. She had a joke book handy in case one of the child performers needed a pun in a pinch for the show. She also rehearsed with her own group of teen dancers, called the "Show Stoppers." The live variety show had helped launch the careers of well-known entertainers including Andrea McArdle, who starred in the first Broadway production of the musical "Annie," and members of Sister Sledge, the 1970s pop group.

After graduating from high school in 1980, at the tender age of fifteen, she enrolled at Temple University in Philadelphia while living at home. She started taking voice classes, modern jazz, and ballet and then switched to psychology and English classes. She then decided to study television and film. She was unfocused in her studies and later realized being in classes with students three years older than her was not the best idea. But like many teenagers at that age, she thought she knew everything. She was still working at the *Al Alberts Showcase,* helping the young girls rehearse before their performances and timing the show for commercial breaks. She wanted to live on her own, but her parents would have none of it. At this point, she was just staying in school because she had to.

"I was very bitter," she said. "I was very sassy."

During summers, she worked as a model and "round-card girl" for boxing matches at resorts and casinos in Atlantic City, where New Jersey residents had legalized gambling only four years earlier. The city was going through a metamorphosis, with prewar resorts being demolished to make way for new, gleaming casino complexes, such as Resorts International, where Donna-Lynne worked. Working as a model meant socializing with the resorts' high rollers in evening gowns at cocktail parties or wearing hot pants and a baseball uniform at themed private gatherings. Celebrities such as movie actor Gene Kelly, opera singer Luciano Pavarotti, boxer Sugar Ray Leonard, and Phillies pitcher Tug McGraw showed up for special events.

The boxing matches could be gruesome, and Donna-Lynne had to sit, expressionless, wearing a sequined top and hot pants, right next to the ring. At times, she would get hit with the blood of a boxer. She learned to discreetly take a hidden towel and wipe it off.

Some people drop out of school to join the circus. In 1984, just shy of twenty years old, Donna-Lynne dropped out of college to join The Muppets. She heard about auditions in New York for a *Sesame Street Live!* show and Sesame Place, a nearby theme park based on Sesame Street characters, and was hired to play "Ernie" and other characters at the park while she continued working in Atlantic City, commuting between both places by bus. It was the beginning of a career portraying characters beloved by children.

She was not at Sesame Place for long. She got invited to go on the road with the "Sesame Street Live!" show soon afterward, and she answered the call. Rehearsals were in Minneapolis, and she went there with a friend from Sesame Place who was from the Twin Cities. She stayed with the woman's family during the six weeks of rehearsals. With her debut in "Sesame Street Live!" just a few days away, Donna-Lynne had an accident that almost sidelined her life as a road performer before it got started. At her friend's house, in the middle of the night, she tripped over a vacuum cleaner while walking in a dark hallway to the bathroom. She broke two toes. For the next few days, she was hobbling around on crutches. But at nineteen, and still below the legal drinking age, she was the baby among the performers, and she did not want to be babied on tour. She wanted to show everyone she was a grown-up, and she insisted on performing. On opening night, she taped her toes together, slipped into her Keystone Kops costume, and cut open the soles of her floppy shoes so her splinted foot would fit. She tossed aside the crutches and performed her act. "The show must go on!" she said.[3]

She was an understudy most of the time, but she moved up, as the tour went on, to become Oscar the Grouch's girlfriend. On her twenty-first birthday, when she could legally drink, she was in Peoria, Illinois, with the tour, and after the show, her castmates treated her to a bottle of Dom Pérignon. Along the way, Donna-Lynne joined the Actors' Equity Association and got her first job as a union representative almost by accident. She became the union representative for the traveling "Sesame Street Live!" show by virtue of having to use the bathroom during a cast meeting. Nobody wanted the job, and when she returned from the restroom during a meeting about who would be the union deputy, she discovered she had been voted to the position in absentia. In her new role, Donna-Lynne made sure the performers had enough personal time between shows. She made sure they were fed and that they were given enough travel time to go from city to city.[4]

Donna-Lynne met her first husband, Joe, on the road with "Sesame Street Live!" He was a truck driver for the concessions business that traveled with the show. Soon, Donna-Lynne got another traveling road show gig with "Snoopy's World of Magic," playing Charlie, Lucy, and Woodstock. Joe, meanwhile, had become a stay-at-home dad when their son, C. J., was born in 1986.

Two years later, after six years on the road, Donna-Lynne left touring and settled down in a north Florida beach town with C. J. and Joe, who had started his own concessions business. He had contracts selling cotton candy and other items at stadiums in Miami and New Orleans. She thought living in Navarre Beach in the Florida Panhandle would give her son some stability.

After Disney announced plans to purchase The Jim Henson Company in 1989, the first full-fledged Muppets attraction—"Here Come the Muppets"—opened at Disney World the following year. The deal was delayed for another fifteen years because of Henson's death that year, but the ties between Disney World and the Muppets were sealed. A fellow performer from Donna-Lynne's Muppets days had moved to Orlando to become a manager for "The Muppets" show at Disney World. The friend started rounding up former performers from the Muppets tour, including Donna-Lynne, to join her at the theme park resort—a putting-the-band-back-together job for the former character performers. And with that, Donna-Lynne headed to Disney World in Orlando.

3

Getting into Character

Like every new Disney World hire, Donna-Lynne had to go through Traditions, a combination of orientation, class, and fraternity or sorority initiation that can last several days. On her first day, a Disney instructor asked Donna-Lynne to remove her makeup and eyeliner. She was not wearing either, so the instructor at "Disney University" told her to wash her face and take out her multiple earrings, which she did. "I wanted to follow the rules, but maybe someone should have warned me about how strict this was going to be," she recalled. It was a preview of Disney's fastidious grooming guidelines.[1]

In the 1990s, a typical Traditions class had several dozen new hires, ready to be inducted into the Disney way of life.[2] Everything they learned was tied to "The Four Keys," a foundational mantra invented by Walt Disney himself that valued "safety, courtesy, show and efficiency." It was a hierarchy, with safety coming first, followed by courtesy, show, and efficiency. Fast-forward three decades, and in spring 2021, Disney added a fifth "key," inclusion, after a year of social justice protests following the death of George Floyd at the hands of a police officer. "Inclusion is essential to our culture and leads us forward as we continue to realize our rich legacy of engaging storytelling, exceptional service and Disney magic," said Josh D'Amaro, chair of Disney Parks, Experiences and Products.[3]

(This addition of a fifth key was one of several reckonings with the social justice protests that Disney made at its theme parks in 2020, as did many companies with decades-old, racially charged brands. In the summer of 2020, Disney changed the Splash Mountain theme park ride over its ties to *Song of the South*, the 1946 movie many viewed as racist. The ride was recast based on *The Princess and the Frog*, a 2009 Disney film with an African American female lead. "The new concept is inclusive—one that all of our guests can connect with and be inspired by, and it speaks to the diversity of the millions of people who visit our parks each year," Disney said at the time).[4]

In the Traditions classes of the 1990s, Donna-Lynne learned about the "7 Guest Service Guidelines"—expected behavior based on those foundational principles that were connected to the Seven Dwarfs. Workers were encouraged to be Happy, to give advice like Doc, to aim to create magical dreams like Sleepy, and to be like Sneezy in spreading the spirit of hospitality. They were warned not to be Bashful, Dopey, or Grumpy.

The new hires mastered Disney trivia—"How tall is Cinderella's Castle? 189 feet." "How many Mickey Mouses are there? Only one, of course!"—so that they were prepared to answer any visitor's questions. They got plastic figurines for answering questions correctly. Most Disney World workers, including Donna-Lynne, still have mementos from their Traditions classes hidden away in bedroom closets across metro Orlando. In the Traditions classes, Donna-Lynne had to learn another vocabulary. She was not an employee who was hired for a job but a "cast member" who had been "cast" for "a role." Dressing rooms and break rooms were "backstage." The people who patrolled the grounds were not security guards but "security hosts." Workers wore "costumes," not uniforms. Starting a work shift was answering "a curtain call." Being out in the public parts of Disney World was being "onstage."

"Regardless of your role, your performance will be on the world's largest stage because all of Walt Disney World is a 27,000-acre stage with the public areas onstage and the 'behind-the-scenes' support area backstage," said an early Disney World employee manual. "Just like any show, we have an audience, not a crowd. Our audience is composed of guests, not customers . . . and we, as cast members, are hosts and hostesses, whether in the Magic Kingdom or a resort-hotel . . . whether onstage or backstage."[5]

Donna-Lynne learned that rides were for amusement parks.[6] Disney World had a series of "adventures and attractions . . . each carefully 'imagineered' and integrated with others to provide the unparalleled Walt Disney World theme show." Every guest was to be treated as a VIP. Workers were encouraged to practice always wearing a friendly smile and using polite phrases such as "May I help you?" and "Have a nice day." Everyone needed to maintain an informal but respectful attitude and refer to each other—even the top bosses—by their first names. "Stuffiness is out," the employee manual said. "We try to keep our sense of humor at all times. . . . You'll be pleasantly surprised how well our internal friendliness among cast members leads to an even greater external friendliness with our guests. In fact, you'll find you're co-starring with the friendliest cast in the world."

Donna-Lynne was told that she would be putting on "a show" for the visitors, and that meant never letting anything ruin the Disney magic by bringing reminders about the real world past the kingdom's gates.[7] That meant never eating, chewing gum, or smoking in front of visitors. "Imagine you're stepping through the castle gates into Fantasyland, only to discover Snow White with a cup of coffee and a cigarette, chatting with other employees about a recent party and football game," the employee manual said. "The destruction of the show is complete and total."

Workers like Donna-Lynne learned that the desire not to shatter any of the fantasy of the Magic Kingdom was a major reason why tunnels existed underneath the Magic Kingdom. In reality, visitors to the Magic Kingdom who walked through Cinderella's Castle or watched a parade on Main Street were on either the second or third floor of the structure, not the first as they might think. Underneath, on the first floor, were the utilidor tunnels that housed break rooms, a cafeteria, walkways, and a trash collection system. The tunnels allowed workers dressed for Frontierland to avoid having to walk through Fantasyland and kept visitors from seeing a worker dressed in a Liberty Square uniform in Adventureland. The tunnels were restricted to employees like Donna-Lynne, but a visitor who inadvertently wandered into them would find flatbed golf carts for transporting materials parked on the side, performers in character costumes walking to their assignments, concrete floors, lockers for workers' street clothes, showers, a hair salon, offices, a library with Disney books and movies, endless racks of uniforms and costumes that the costume department handed out to workers each day, and walls painted with the signs indicating which "lands" were directly upstairs. The decor was utilitarian, and there were endless pipes running against the wall carrying the theme park's garbage through the tunnels that looped underneath the park.

The tunnels also had rooms where the performers could stretch out and warm up before going "upstairs."[8] Warm-up coaches made sure the performers were prepared for moving around in a costume that weighed anywhere from twenty to forty pounds. They had break rooms where the character performers could relax for a half hour with their costume heads off before going back outside into scorching Florida heat and sweltering humidity.

When she was at the Magic Kingdom, Donna-Lynne would get overwhelmed by the tunnels and always seemed to get lost in them. "There are so many staircases," she said. "Sometimes you go up, thinking you're on the right one, and you end up in the middle of a kitchen."

The Traditions course was sometimes held in classrooms fitted with mounted photos on the wall of Disney's various divisions.[9] There, workers like Donna-Lynne learned about the company's history and its wide range of operations—from television and consumer products to the theme parks. After their time in the classroom, new hires like Donna-Lynne were escorted as a class into the Magic Kingdom, where they would walk around the park as their instructors pointed out examples of safety, courtesy, show, and efficiency. They ate lunch in a cafeteria in the tunnels. Disney's unions were given the opportunity during the orientation to tell new workers what they did and encourage them to become members. On the third day of Traditions, someone from the department where the new hires would be working came to the classroom to pick them up. They were taken to the costuming department, where they got uniforms based on their size and which area of the parks they were working. They changed in a locker room and returned their uniforms to the costuming department each night to be laundered. In the parks, a supervisor wrote up a training plan for each new worker. If the new hire worked in food services, the plan might include taking a class on food safety. If they worked in a retail shop, they might take a class on how to work the shops' registers and how to handle money. As Disney World grew over the decades, more workers were needed, and Disney did not have the luxury of hiring only people who were sold on the magic of the place. They had to hire people who looked at it as a job, not a mission.

Author Cher Krause Knight described this change over decades in the types of workers that were hired, and their attenuated devotion to the traditional Disney norms, as a "quiet revolution" at Disney World. "Workers of the past seemed to abide more fully by Disney's party line," Knight writes in *Power and Paradise in Walt Disney's World.* "Today's employees are less content to be hemmed in by the strictures of Disneyism, echoed in training handbooks professing, 'We hope that you enjoy thinking our way.' . . . Thus, while they perform their jobs, wear their uniforms and recite their scripts, more and more of Disney's employees have reclaimed varying degrees of personal individuality, an evolution that was endorsed—at least in part—by the company."[10]

But the character performers seemed to maintain the traditional, mission-focused Disney magic more than the parks' other workers since they were required to bring the characters to life. Their positions required auditions, and the roles often were allocated based on performers' height and weight. A performer had to be small to play Mickey Mouse, Lilo, or one of the Seven Dwarfs. A performer needed to be over six feet tall to be Goofy or Captain Hook. Typically, a new hire would have to be a "fur character," that is, in a head-to-toe costume, before they could be a "face character" like a princess. Inside the costumes, gender was unimportant, and most times women played Mickey Mouse. The Disney managers leading the auditions wanted to see how a potential character performer could move, with co-ordination and high energy at the top of their list of qualities they desired. Performers auditioning to be characters were given simple dance routines, and casting directors rated them using colored cards. Red was the highest-rated review, followed by yellow, blue, and green. The want-to-be characters also had to tell a story through pantomime and could not use words. Per-formers who received red and yellow cards during auditions were allowed to participate in Disney's famous parades.

New hires being trained to be costumed performers also had to learn the unique signature of their characters so it would be consistent across differ-ent performers and over time in the autograph books of the young visitors to the Disney parks.[11] The performers-in-training were given binders with the character signatures, and they practiced writing their characters' names, over and over again, in costumed gloves. Toward the end of the training, the new hires were brought in their costumes before managers in a room. In most cases, it was the first time they were wearing their head and body costumes together, and they walked in a circle for several minutes. The costumes could make the performers feel like they were in astronaut suits walking on the surface of the moon. Movements did not feel normal in the costumes. Over the years, the performers' bodies often conformed to the costumes to the point where performers who played Pluto or Goofy would hunch over from years of children grabbing onto their noses and pulling on their necks.

If a new hire passed that walking-in-a-circle test, they were considered ready to go out into the parks in costume.[12] The new hires had rules to learn. Children were not allowed to sit in their laps. Performers were not allowed to hold babies and, whenever possible, they must kneel down to the children's eye level. Performers were not allowed to tell friends or family members that they played a particular character since that would ruin the magic. Instead, they referred to themselves as "friends" of the characters they played.

Once out in the parks, if performers became ill, got injured, or lost parts of their costumes, they were supposed to alert their escorts by raising their hands to their eyes as a sign of distress. Character performers who became ill on the job were encouraged to remain in costume until emergency aid arrived or they could get "backstage," but they would not be punished for removing their costumes. "A change of clothing . . . shall be provided as soon as possible," according to the contract.[13]

Performers who had started their careers as Disney princesses often graduated into more mature roles, such as Mary Poppins or the fairy god-mother. Seniority often carried the day in Disney management decisions except when it came to casting for a show or parade. In those cases, man-agers could hire people based solely on talent. If new shows were in pro-duction, character performers could schedule auditions or put their names on "interest sheets" that indicated they wanted to get a look from a show director or choreographer.[14] Winning the highly coveted "face" roles also came with premium pay. By the 2010s, performers who played well-known characters like Cinderella or Peter Pan got an additional $3.25 an hour, on top of their usual wages.

Because Cinderella, Aladdin, and the other "face" characters could be played by either Teamsters or Equity members, depending on whether or not they had speaking or singing roles, the two unions had reached an agreement hammering out which type of roles went to members of each union. Singers or actors in a parade or a show with a script and a plot, dance ensembles of stage shows, and "atmosphere" actors interacting with visitors in the parks were Equity members. Characters working in parades and doing "meet-and-greets" with visitors were Teamsters. Occasionally, a Teamsters member would have to substitute for an Equity member in a pinch if they played the same character. If there were any disagreements about whether a part should be Equity or Teamsters, they would be settled by a committee made up of representatives from each union and Disney. If all else failed, the disputes would be settled by an outside arbitrator.

For the performers, the costumes could feel awkward. For one performer playing the Tigger character from Winnie-the-Pooh, who was criminally charged with touching the breast of a thirteen-year-old girl while posing for a photo at the Magic Kingdom, the bulkiness of the character costumes ended up being the saving grace. During Michael Chartrand's trial in 2004, his Orlando-based attorney, who also moonlighted as Goofy and Tigger at Disney World, insisted that the Tigger costume be left in the jury room so jurors could try it on. During closing arguments of the trial, in an only-in-Orlando moment, defense attorney Jeffrey Kaufman brought the Tig-ger costume into the courtroom and pulled it out of its box. He told the jurors, "This is my friend, Tigger. It might spoil the magic for most people. You know?" The defense attorney then proceeded to strap on Tigger's tail. Kaufman placed a cloth around his neck and put on the enormous orange-and-black-striped head. He then placed two large orange mitts on his hands to show the jurors how the costume limits peripheral vision and arm movements. The gambit worked. Jurors who smirked when Kaufman tried on the costume acquitted Chartrand of lewd and lascivious molestation, agreeing with defense arguments that, if he did touch the breast, it was accidental. The character performer was spared the prospect of spending up to fifteen years in prison had he been convicted.[15]

The character performers were required to undergo at least one audition a year to make sure they were still suited to their characters. Managers checked the performers' body shape and general appearance to make sure they still had the right look. "In situations where an employee exceeds the size limitations of the costume . . . the company will make reasonable efforts to transfer such employee," the contract said.[16]

Camaraderie was strong among the character performers, especially among the veterans who had worked in the Disney parks for decades and regarded each other as work family members. Decreased enthusiasm among newer hires came with Disney World's continuing breakneck expansion. That never-ending growth also resulted in a more regimented implementation of its rules since it would be impossible to handle a workforce of tens of thousands of employees without a strict organizational structure. "It used to be fun, but now it's a business," lamented one longtime character performer, Melanie Polson. "Back then, they used to hire quality people, but now they hire anybody."[17] Over the years, Donna-Lynne would see workers take jobs at the parks for reasons more practical than the "Disney magic." "I think some workers buy the pixie dust and they want the magic that they watched on *The Wonderful World of Disney* years ago," said Donna-Lynne, referring to the long-running television series. "Other people are just there for the medical insurance."[18]

After going through Traditions, Donna-Lynne headed straight to rehearsals for the "Here Come the Muppets" show. But she could not find the right rehearsals studio. Outside, at a smoking table beside one of the rehearsal bungalows at Hollywood Studios, she ran into two veteran character performers who asked her name. One of them initially thought she said, "Donovan," so that became Donna-Lynne's new nickname, and she even got a name tag with that moniker as a joke.

As a performer, Donna-Lynne drew her motivation from connecting with other performers and creating an energy of joy and fun in their dancing and movements. There were magical moments at unexpected times working at the theme parks, such as seeing the Magic Kingdom peaceful and devoid of crowds in the predawn hours after a night of exhausting rehearsals for a new show or parade. Everything from Cinderella's Castle to the storefronts along Main Street, U.S.A. seemed to glow silently against the night. On those nights, Donna-Lynne and the other performers would find somewhere on the resort's property—in the tunnels under the Magic Kingdom, a trailer behind-the-scenes, or a warehouse that housed the parade floats—to crash for a few hours before reporting for their day shifts.

Donna-Lynne had worked at Disney World for a year before she realized, in 1992, that the character performers were Teamsters. No one had told her that before. She was in the greenroom of the "Little Mermaid" show, where performers wait before going onstage, when someone backstage told her she had a phone call. On the line was the business agent for the character performers saying he had heard from some of the former Muppets performers that she had been an effective Equity deputy while on tour. He asked if she would be interested in being a Teamsters steward for the character performers. Donna-Lynne decided she needed to join the union first. She met with the business agent, signed a membership card, and took a look at the contract. Reviewing it, she saw omissions and items that needed to be corrected. She decided that they really could use her help.

Donna-Lynne eventually became an assistant business agent, which allowed her to continue working as a performer at Disney World but with greater on-site union responsibilities. In 1999, she was asked to become a full-time business agent for the character performers, meaning she would be employed by the Teamsters and take a leave of absence from Disney World. Though she did not know it at the time, that leave of absence would last almost two decades. Once again, she came to the job almost by accident. She was supposed to work as a business agent for a limited time, only half a year, while the business agent she was temporarily substituting for tried to expunge an old drug charge from his record so he could be a representative for the Teamsters local. He got the charge expunged. But the president of the union affiliate at the time, Mario Ferenac, decided not to bring him back, under the belief he would not be getting the business agent's support in an upcoming election for Local 385. Donna-Lynne was the first performer to become a business agent for the characters. Ferenac was a well-dressed, handsome man whose smoothness polished off the rough Teamsters edges. Upon hiring her, he said that he could not pay her the same as a man. Men getting paid more than women at the Teamsters "just became the norm," she said.

Donna-Lynne took the job anyway, both because she wanted to represent her fellow performers and because, at the age of thirty-five, her performing days were numbered. Being a dancer and performer at Disney World was accompanied by residual pain in the back and neck. Although some Disney dancers worked into their fifties, the typical age to stop was in their thirties, as it became harder for the body to adjust to the pulls and strains. After dancing in the streets of Disney World, Donna-Lynne was now headed to the local Teamsters union hall.

4

The Rat's Nest

Joining the Teamsters management was like landing on another planet for Donna-Lynne. The Teamsters, in return, regarded her as an alien in their musty, two-story, midcentury Local 385 union hall. She was used to constant change on the job, whether it was learning a new dance routine or playing a different Disney character. The Teamsters were all about routines, whether in their shift work, driving the same route, or going to the same warehouse. The Teamsters members worked in industries that were overwhelmingly male—truck-driving and warehousing. The character performers were theater geeks, with women and large numbers of gay men in their ranks. An overwhelming majority of the performers had gone to college and had theatrical backgrounds, so there was some resentment from the former truckers in the Teamsters union hall over what they perceived as the performers' charmed lives. The performers, often referred to as "entertainment," were diverse, expressive, creative, and perhaps the most persuasive purveyors of Disney's fantasy world. The Teamsters leaders at Local 385 regarded the character performers Donna-Lynne represented as not having "real" jobs. The local Teamsters leaders in the union hall often referred to Donna-Lynne's members as "a bunch of queers" who "pretended it was Halloween every day" and got to play "dress-up" to go to work.[1]

"Characters are a very unique group," said John "Spike" Coskey, a former Local 385 business agent for Disney World's warehouse workers and drivers. "They have their own language. It's hard to understand entertainment. First of all, they think they're all on Broadway. They have a lot of egos. If you're a dancer or actor, they don't want to be represented by a truck driver. They don't want to hear from a truck driver about dancing. They don't want to hear from a truck driver about face characters. So, we decided to keep Donna-Lynne. She had a background as a performer."[2] But that did not mean the other Local 385 leaders liked Donna-Lynne. Not long into her tenure, someone placed a note on her office door in the Teamsters' hall. "Jesus may love you, but I think you're a fucking cunt," it read.

Within months of joining the Teamsters full-time, Donna-Lynne was swamped by the dirty politics of the local, which Spike had dubbed "the rat's nest." To understand the pickle Donna-Lynne had gotten into, it helps to know about the modern history of the Teamsters, unionism in the United States, and the nine-thousand-member Local 385 in Orlando.

First, the history lesson. At the beginning of the twentieth century, a handful of corporations possessed immense concentrations of financial power. Two hundred of the nation's largest corporations controlled about half of all corporate assets by 1929. Economic devastation from the Great Depression caused a rethinking of the nation's economic structures, and President Franklin Delano Roosevelt's administration, and a willing Congress in 1933, put into law in the National Industrial Recovery Act the right of employees to organize and bargain. As Nelson Lichtenstein notes in his book *State of the Union,* the ability to organize and bargain collectively was akin to a civil rights movement in the workforce. In the following decade, the growth of unions went hand in hand with the New Deal policies of Roosevelt's administration. Lichtenstein writes, "A huge proportion of all those who became unionists during the 1930s and 1940s were African Americans, Mexican Americans or from European immigrant families. For them, the New Deal and the new unionism represented not just a higher standard of living, but a doorway that opened onto the democratic promise of American life." They offered the material promise of trading in work boots for the comforts of slippers every evening in a home that one owned, in a neighborhood safe enough to raise children. "Security constituted not just freedom, but a social, psychological fortress from which to challenge illegitimate power, both on the job and off," Lichtenstein writes. In asserting their rights through strikes and other actions in the 1930s, these unions and their members believed they were democratizing a labor relationship with their employers. On the other hand, those employers, more often than not, responded to the changing circumstances with violent attacks with the help of corporate militias and the support of the police.[3]

The International Brotherhood of Teamsters, Chauffeurs, Stablemen and Helpers was formed in 1903 from the merger of two unions representing horse-team drivers, the Team Drivers International Union and the Teamsters National Union.[4] The Teamsters had a long history with organized crime, dating back to the 1920s and 1930s. Throughout the country, mob bosses were embedded as officers in Teamsters locals. By the mid-1950s, organized crime leaders had helped elevate Jimmy Hoffa to the top leadership post at the International Brotherhood of Teamsters, a move that caused the American Federation of Labor and Congress of Industrial Organizations to expel the Teamsters from its umbrella labor federation. As the Teamsters' top leader, Hoffa centralized power in the union, shifting it away from local drivers. "While he was a popular and charismatic leader, Hoffa was also a union boss, a dictator who tolerated no opposition," Dan La Botz writes in *Rank and File Rebellion.*[5]

Hoffa's consolidation of power and his strongman persona became a template for antidemocratic tendencies that would haunt the Teamsters in the following decades. "He crushed local unions that fought for their autonomy and destroyed rank-and-file movements that rose to fight against him," La Botz writes. "But worse still, Hoffa gave the Teamsters members the appearance of power and the swagger of self-confidence while depriving them of the only possible source of real confidence, the control of their own union."[6]

By the 1980s, the Mafia had control over many key officials at all levels of the Teamsters organization, sometimes through violence. Several mobsters treated local unions as their personal piggy banks. Over the decades, several Teamsters presidents had faced criminal indictments, starting with the first Teamsters president, Cornelius Shea, who served five years in prison for attempting to murder his mistress in 1909. Jimmy Hoffa had gone to prison in 1964 for jury tampering and attempted bribery after federal prosecutors said he used the Teamsters pension fund to make loans to mob-controlled hotels, casinos, and shopping malls. After Hoffa's prison sentence was commuted by President Richard Nixon, Hoffa campaigned to run again for president of the Teamsters against the wishes of the Mafia, who believed his successor was more open to their influence. Hoffa was last seen in the parking lot of a restaurant in suburban Detroit, and it is widely assumed that Mafia henchmen killed him.[7]

Hoffa's predecessor as Teamsters president, David Beck, was convicted in 1957 of embezzlement and federal income tax evasion. Three different Teamsters presidents with mob ties in the 1970s and 1980s were either investigated or indicted on charges including extortion, racketeering, and conspiring to bribe a US senator from Nevada. In many of the cases, top Teamsters officials ratted each other out as informants and witnesses to federal investigators in exchange for getting better deals themselves.[8]

Meanwhile, the Teamsters as an international union had acquired great wealth. Its headquarters, located just across the plaza from the US Senate, was called the "Marble Palace" for a reason. At one time, the Marble Palace employed a French chef who Kennedy administration officials tried to lure away but failed to because the White House could not match the union's pay. There had been two Gulfstream jets available to whisk away Teamsters officials to anywhere in the United States, including one with a fully stocked bar and a bathroom with gold-plated faucets and a marble sink. Two full-time pilots were kept on the union's payroll.[9]

The modern Teamsters era began in 1988 when the federal government sued the union, alleging they not only were in bed with the Cosa Nostra organized crime syndicate but were "a wholly owned subsidiary of organized crime."[10] A civil lawsuit against nineteen current and former Teamsters officials and twenty-six reputed mobsters or associates was a landmark case, not to mention a daring move, led by Rudy Giuliani, then the US attorney in New York. Giuliani and his lawyers not only sued the nation's largest and most famous union at the time, as well as the largest criminal organization, but it was the first time a racketeering lawsuit had been filed against an international union. The lawsuit said the Mafia, abetted by the Teamsters leaders who did their bidding, violated rank-and-file members' rights to democratically elect their union leaders. They did this by playing key roles in the selection of Teamsters general presidents. The lawsuit also said that members were denied economic benefits from the union's assets and investments, which the Mafia used as their personal bank. The lawsuit claimed the Mafia was able to exert political influence through the Teamsters and use the union's pension as a bank in the form of loans that were never repaid.[11] Basically, the federal prosecutors wanted to end corruption in the international union and make it more democratic for its members.

In the following months, the Teamsters reached a watershed settlement with the federal prosecutors, which was the biggest step toward union democracy in the Teamsters' history. The agreement called for democratic elections supervised by an independent officer for the first time. The Teamsters also agreed to follow new rules aimed at eliminating corruption and ending any Mafia associations. Violations were investigated, prosecuted, and punished by an investigations officer and an independent administrator. The Teamsters agreed to pay the salaries of an elections officer, an independent administrator, and an investigations officer. The independent administrator and the investigations officer supervising the Teamsters were succeeded in 1991 by a three-member Independent Review Board (IRB). "The government and the Teamster reform movement both felt that this agreement would make it possible to break the stranglehold of the Mafia on the union," La Botz writes in *Rank and File Rebellion*.[12]

The agreement led to the expulsion or suspension of hundreds of Teamsters officers, the ousting of the leadership of dozens of local unions, and the temporary taking over of the leadership reins over dozens of local unions by the International Brotherhood of Teamsters in a process known as trusteeship.[13] It also led to the banishment of the International Brotherhood of Teamsters top brass, including General President Jackie Presser and General Secretary Weldon Mathis.

One of the milestones of this democratic transition into the modern Teamsters took place in Orlando in June 1991 when the Teamsters held a historic international convention in the Florida city where members for the first time picked delegates who would then select candidates for the top offices.[14] Later that year, in a secret-ballot election supervised by the court-appointed elections officer, the Teamsters elected as their leader insurgent candidate Ron Carey in the first direct election of the International Brotherhood of Teamsters. Carey, who made battling corruption a key component of his campaign, was helped by a split in the Teamsters establishment vote between two other candidates.[15] Carey had the backing of Teamsters for a Democratic Union, a reformist caucus of rank-and-file members that often opposed the Teamsters leadership by pushing for more transparency, accountability, and democratic measures. Founded in the 1970s almost as an internal opposition party to the Teamsters leadership, the TDU was often viewed with contempt by some rank-and-file Teamsters who smeared them as leftists or socialists. Nevertheless, Carey won with their support. Carey promised to sell the International Brotherhood of Teamsters' fleet of jets, stop officials from receiving multiple salaries from different boards or locals, and shrink the size of the union's bureaucracy.

After Carey's election, the Independent Review Board (IRB) assumed investigative and disciplinary responsibilities from the investigative officer and the independent administrator. The IRB was charged with investigating organized crimes and scrutinizing high-ranking International Brotherhood of Teamsters officials. For the lower-level local unions, an investigator would be tasked with probing allegations of malfeasance and then sending an investigative report to the three-member IRB. If the IRB approved the investigator's recommended disciplinary charge, the case would be sent to the local union or joint council for discipline, with the IRB given the last word on whether the disciplinary action taken by the local union or joint council was appropriate. Final approval came from the federal judge overseeing the settlement between the federal government and leaders of the International Brotherhood of Teamsters.

Almost from the start of the IRB's existence, the International Brotherhood of Teamsters was set on proving the IRB was not needed to monitor union affairs against corruption and mob influence. Carey set up an internal committee that was supposed to investigate the union and its locals for corruption and mismanagement in an effort to usurp the role of the IRB. But critics saw it as a weapon Carey used to go after his opponents.

One of the great tools the IRB had against corrupt local affiliates was the ability to recommend that the International Brotherhood of Teamsters' general president impose a trusteeship on corrupt or mismanaged locals. A trusteeship allowed the general president to take over the management of the local by replacing the local president with a new, temporary leader called a "trustee." The trustee was charged with cleaning house and then setting in place elections so that members could choose new leaders.

By the beginning of the twenty-first century, the Teamsters were one of the largest unions in the world, with 1.4 million members in North America across hundreds of affiliates, known as "locals." In many ways, the Teamsters were set up the way the nation's major political parties are structured: With the political parties, there were local Democratic and Republican chapters, state parties, and then the national headquarters. With the Teamsters, there were locals, joint councils made up of three or more locals, and the international headquarters in Washington, DC, where the president presided.[16]

The locals were the backbone of the Teamsters, negotiating contracts and providing business agents to represent workers on their jobs.[17] Members of the local affiliates elected their own officers and voted on their own rules. Local presidents often wielded great power, assigning positions, managing budgets, and deciding on charitable or political donations.

In 1996, Carey ran for reelection as the Teamsters general president, but this time he faced James Hoffa, an attorney who was the son of the legendary former Teamsters leader, Jimmy Hoffa. James Hoffa was cut from a very different mold from that of his father and other Teamster leaders—more brains, less brawn. He held an undergraduate degree in economics and was a graduate of the University of Michigan Law School. Hoffa had built a successful career as a labor lawyer before deciding to run against the then incumbent general president of the union in the 1990s.

Carey's campaign focused on his efforts to eliminate scores of corrupt leaders from the union, and he pointed to the fact that he had put into trusteeship almost seventy corrupt or mismanaged local unions. He sold off the union's jets, cut his salary, and fired the French chef who worked at the Marble Palace. But only a small number of local unions were loyal to Carey.[18]

One of them was Local 385 in Orlando, and Donna-Lynne in 1996 was sent to the Teamsters' convention in Philadelphia as an alternate delegate for Carey. At the time, Donna-Lynne did not have strong feelings one way or another for either Carey or Hoffa. Even though she would not be a Teamsters official for another three years—she was just a member working as a performer at Disney World—the local had her run as an alternate delegate to the convention to be a "fresh face"—that is, someone meant to demonstrate that the Teamsters were not just a bunch of burly truck drivers. She won with 547 votes, the most of any Local 385 candidate on the ballot for picking delegates and alternate delegates, including the local's top officers.[19]

The stakes for the election were high, and it brought out intra-union fighting between supporters of Carey and backers of Hoffa.[20] Local 385 members backing opposing candidates filed a half dozen complaints against each other with the elections officer, alleging some delegates were not qualified to go to the convention or saying that the then head of Local 385, Danny "Pete" Peterson, only allowed pro-Carey literature at the union hall and prohibited pro-Hoffa flyers. The elections officer ordered Hoffa literature to be placed in the Orlando union hall and said that campaigning could not be prohibited in the union hall's adjacent parking lot.

While campaigning for general president of the International Brotherhood of Teamsters, Hoffa did not shy away from the association with his father, who was still popular among rank-and-file Teamster members. He disputed that Carey had eliminated corruption from the Teamsters and vowed to end the consent decree allowing the US government to oversee the Teamsters' business. At the convention, he unsuccessfully proposed eliminating the general president's ability to impose trusteeships on local unions. Although it failed, such a move would have sacrificed an important tool for rooting out corruptions in locals.[21]

During a vote-by-mail election in December 1996, Carey defeated Hoffa with 52 percent of the vote. Not long afterward, the independent elections officer overseeing the vote noticed several suspiciously large donations to a Carey fundraising committee. Further investigation revealed a scheme in which the Teamsters agreed to donate to political organizations whose wealthy supporters in turn donated to Carey's reelection campaign. The elections officer refused to certify the election and she ordered a new election. A subsequent elections officer disqualified Carey from running in the new election, and in 1998 the IRB expelled him from the Teamsters. In a weird twist of fate, James Hoffa became the general president, a position he would hold for the next two and a half decades.

A grand jury indicted Carey on making false statements and perjury charges in 2001. According to a congressional report, the net worth of the Teamsters under Carey's leadership had dropped from more than $150 million to $20 million, due to unchecked spending, forcing the union to impose a dues assessment on rank-and-file members.[22]

When James Hoffa became president, there was concern about the direction the Teamsters would go. Would the union continue down the path of reform that had started with the consent decree with Giuliani, or would Hoffa follow in his father's footsteps? One of Hoffa's goals was to free the Teamsters of the consent decree, and he figured the only way he could do that was to prove the union was serious about keeping out mob influences. To accomplish that, he created an internal anti-corruption program that would monitor and eliminate any elements of fraud or criminal behavior. Called Project RISE, it was led by a former federal prosecutor. The program was criticized for lacking independent enforcement powers. By 2004, frustrated at what they saw as Teamsters leadership stymieing their investigations, the former prosecutor and other staffers and members of an advisory board for the Project RISE program resigned. The end of Project RISE dealt a blow to the Teamsters' near-term goal to get out from under the supervision of the federal government's oversight.[23]

It took another decade before the Teamsters started the process of freeing itself from direct government oversight. In 2015, federal prosecutors in New York agreed to start a five-year process in which the government would relinquish its supervision of Teamsters' affairs. The 2015 agreement said there had been "significant success in eliminating corruption from within the IBT (International Brotherhood of Teamsters) and in conducting free, open and democratic elections for its International Officers and Convention Delegates."

But even with all the reforms since the consent decree decades earlier, the Teamsters could be undemocratic. In 2019, tens of thousands of Teamsters voted down a five-year contract agreement with UPS, one of the largest collective bargaining contracts in the United States. Despite the rejection by its members, Teamsters officials invoked an obscure rule to get the contract approved. According to the rule, in votes when less than half of eligible members participate, a rejection requires two-thirds of participants to vote down the contract. Only 54 percent of the ballots were "no," so the Teamster's leadership approved the contract, even though a majority of the rank-and-file who voted had opposed it.

"This destroys a union," said Sean Mason, a UPS driver in Orlando who was a member of Local 385. "They had 54 percent of the people vote no and they ignored the vote."[24]

Among the targets of the IRB in eliminating corruption in the Teamsters following the consent decree with the federal government in the early 1990s was the head of Local 385 in Orlando. Larry Parker, who led the local affiliate from 1982 to 1993, was accused by investigators of taking thousands of dollars in kickbacks from members who worked in the film industry. According to investigators, members who worked on films being made in central Florida were encouraged to give "donations" or "campaign contributions" to Parker or a surrogate, even if there was no campaign going on or he was running unopposed, in order to secure their jobs. Parker's surrogates collected anywhere from $4,800 to $8,400 from crew members working as drivers on the films *Doc Hollywood, Days of Thunder, Passenger 57,* and *Wilder Napalm.*[25]

Parker would personally make the selection of who worked on which movies in central Florida, so union members felt like they would not get hired on film sets if they did not make contributions of several hundred dollars to Parker. "I never questioned because sometimes if you questioned it, you didn't, you know, look good in the eyes of the local," one Local 385 member told investigators. Another Local 385 member who worked on the Wesley Snipes movie *Passenger 57* said he did not think it was fair since he had been a union member almost a quarter century, but he gave anyway since he had been out of work and did it "to keep peace in the family." A third Local 385 member who worked on the Tom Cruise film *Days of Thunder* said she never worked in the film industry again after she refused to give a "campaign contribution" to Parker. A fourth member testified, "You either paid it or you didn't work."

Local 385 voted Larry Parker out the leadership in late 1993, but he had one parting gift for colleagues and the members of his executive team who were departing with him. He got them jobs at a television show, *Thunder in Paradise.* Old habits die hard, and he also asked a surrogate to ask the union members working on the show for money. One Teamster on the show told investigators, "I wasn't too happy about, you know, driving a 10-year-old Ford pickup truck and giving money to a guy that was driving a brand-new Suburban. Seems like he'd probably be in a good enough position to pay off his own bills." When investigators questioned Parker about what he used the money for, he said, "I used some of it for campaign expenses and some of it for living expenses." But a surrogate, who was a captain for the Teamsters on the television show, told investigators that the campaign debt had been paid off, so the money went straight to Parker. The investigators recommended that Parker be permanently barred from the International Brotherhood of Teamsters and that he lose his health insurance and pension fund.

In the case of Local 385, the apple did not fall far from the tree. Parker's father, Paul Parker, who was the local union's first president when it was chartered in 1968, had gone to prison for bombings against companies in central Florida that refused to recognize that the Teamsters represented their workers.[26] Workers at the Keystone Trucking Company and Overland Hauling Company had voted to certify the Teamsters as their union, but when the companies refused to recognize the union as their bargaining unit, they voted to strike in February 1971. Without much progress being made on the strike, Paul Parker told associates he wanted the unit to "rain dynamite" on the two companies in order to increase the pressure. A bomb exploded a few weeks later at Keystone Trucking Company. That was followed by an explosion at the Municipal Justice Building weeks later, and then a second bombing at the Keystone Trucking Company that damaged trucks. A few weeks later, two associates of Paul Parker bombed the offices of the Overland Hauling Company. They were pulled over and arrested two-tenths of a mile from the company's offices by federal agents who witnessed what had happened from an observation post across the street.

Paul Parker was arrested in 1976, just a few hours before the five-year statute of limitations on the crimes ran out. On subsequent appeals, though, his attorneys argued his arrest took place outside the statute of limitations because there were two leap years during that five-year period. His arrest on aiding and abetting others in damaging a building and conspiracy occurred so many years after the crimes because it took years for his former associates, who had been convicted at earlier trials, to cooperate and agree to testify against him. He was convicted on all three counts and sentenced to ten years in prison. Although Paul Parker was convicted in 1976, he did not enter prison until three years later, when he had exhausted his appeals. In the meantime, he stayed on as president of Local 385.

Fighting over the leadership of the International Brotherhood of Teamsters trickled down to local union affiliates like Local 385. Larry Parker, who was president in 1991 during the first general election after the 1989 consent decree, supported R. V. Durham for general president and opposed Carey. But his successors, Danny "Pete" Peterson and Mario Ferenac, supported Carey, and eventually they took over the local union leadership, in 1994, running as reform candidates.[27] Carey, who was then the general president, was so grateful for their support that he flew into Orlando to swear them in.

During the campaign to lead Local 385, Peterson, who won as president, and Ferenac, who assumed the vice president job, portrayed Parker as being out of touch with rank-and-file members. By then, like many successful Teamsters local presidents, Larry Parker had spent the past decade climbing the ranks of the International Brotherhood of Teamsters organization on the national stage, working as a representative, a director of the convention trade division, and a coordinator for the 1991 international convention while maintaining his duties with Local 385. Peterson and Ferenac portrayed themselves as agents of change who were ready to shake up the old guard. The new local leaders won because "they had a message the membership wanted to hear, a message of fundamental democratic principles," Carey said during the swearing in of Local 385's new leaders.[28]

By the mid-1990s, Local 385 had been established in central Florida for a quarter of a century, and as happens with many labor organizations, labor agitation like the illegal deeds of Paul Parker had been replaced with bureaucracy.[29] The Teamsters local had become a well-oiled machine of collecting dues and negotiating contracts, if not necessarily listening to the concerns of members. The local was administering up to fifty-five collective bargaining agreements across several industries and on behalf of nine thousand workers. With their six-figure salaries, union-paid cars, and annual Teamster trips to Las Vegas, the leaders of Local 385 also were leading a lifestyle foreign to many of their rank-and-file members, particularly theme park workers who sometimes lived paycheck to paycheck.

These types of benefits for union leaders often raise red flags about union democracy's health in a local, according to Ashby, a labor scholar. "The idea seeps into the soul of even the best leaders that 'I deserve the best. I work hard for this union. I am responsible for thousands of people,'" Ashby writes. "Union officials start to think they should wear expensive clothes because they negotiate with corporate lawyers and officials who wear expensive clothes. They start to think that they, too, should have huge houses in wealthy suburbs. They start to think that they, too, should have the latest models of leased luxury cars."[30]

Throughout the 1990s, there was constant internecine fighting in Local 385 between supporters of different candidates for general president of the International Brotherhood of Teamsters. They took the form of petty, yet vicious, tit-for-tat complaints filed with the elections' office over alleged campaign violations. Those complaints were over whether campaign literature was illegally posted or whether union resources were improperly used on behalf of an International candidate. The Teamster local affiliates often were used as proxies in the battle for control of the Teamsters Union waged by the candidates for general president.

Donna-Lynne found herself in the middle of one of those proxy fights when she joined the Teamsters full-time in 1999 as a business agent.[31] Because Local 385's leaders had been so pro-Carey, Hoffa, once he assumed office, sent an international representative down to Florida as payback to look into any potential shenanigans in the union local. Ferenac—a Carey supporter, after all—thought Donna-Lynne had become too chummy with the pro-Hoffa Teamsters representative, Jim Blanchard. Plus, Donna-Lynne refused to run on Ferenac's slate for the next local elections because he would not pay her the same as a man. So, Donna-Lynne became the subject of a US Department of Labor investigation, which she blamed Ferenac for instigating, over whether she was using a Disney discount given to employees to win favor with Blanchard and his wife during their Florida stay. Donna-Lynne was still considered a Disney employee, just one on extended leave to work for the union, and she was entitled to the same discounts for family and friends as other Disney workers. At one point, she recalled, a Department of Labor investigator met her at a Denny's restaurant for an interview with the goal of trying to get her to admit she had paid for gifts at Disney World for the Teamsters investigator and his wife. The investigator apparently had pulled her credit card information and told her that he could find out what kind of underwear she was buying at Victoria's Secret. That creeped her out and made her feel gross, but she refused to be intimidated by him.

The investigation eventually was dropped.

5

All Politics Is Local

The first time John "Spike" Coskey laid eyes on Donna-Lynne at the union hall, he thought she was the biggest snob. By this time, in the late 1990s, they were both Local 385 shop stewards—she for the character performers, and he for warehouse workers and drivers at Disney World. They met during a stewards' meeting at the Local 385 union hall, before Donna-Lynne had become a business representative. Donna-Lynne had spent all night at rehearsals and had rushed to the union hall for a morning meeting. She needed to get back for the start of "The Hunchback of Notre Dame" show at Disney World and did not have time to chitchat after the meeting. Spike felt like she had blown him off and was acting like she was too good for him, which was typical of how drivers viewed the character performers in their union. But they got to know each other over the next year, and after another meeting at the union hall, as they walked to their cars in the parking lot, he told her, "You know? You're all right."[1]

Spike thought Donna-Lynne was more than "all right." Soon, they started a ten-year on-again, off-again relationship that produced their son, Austin. They never lived together.

Spike was a burly, fun-loving native of the Philadelphia area who came from a Teamsters family. His father, brother, and uncle had worked in Teamsters jobs as drivers and dispatchers for the *Philadelphia Inquirer*. In the late 1980s, fresh on his own, Spike moved to Orlando. With few job prospects, his father told him to go to the Teamsters' hall and ask for a job. He ended up working construction at Boardwalk and Baseball, a baseball-themed park that opened in 1987 but closed three years later. From there, Spike poured concrete for a company before moving on to construction plumbing at two of the premier hotels being built at Walt Disney World, the Swan and the Dolphin. Spike and members of his crew working on the construction of the Dolphin were nonunion. Every day, union workers would pass out flyers to the nonunion workers, advertising that they got paid more than the nonunion crew. The construction unions were upset that Disney was using nonunion labor, claiming it violated the resort's contract with the unions. But Disney responded that they had no control over whether union or nonunion workers were hired, since the hotel was being built and financed by third parties. This was a somewhat tense time for labor relations at the theme park resort because contractors were using nonunion labor. The anger at one contractor, Aoki Corp., was tinged with nationalism and racism, as the company was Japanese. At a rally in May 1988, hundreds of union workers picketed outside the construction site. At some point, some of the protesters tore down part of the site's fence, overturned a Toyota car parked in a lot, and smashed the car with sledgehammers in a symbolic gesture against Japanese business.[2]

Spike had been blabbing to fellow workers about what the union workers were getting paid and had set up a meeting with union officials about organizing the workers at the Dolphin, but he got fired when word got out to his managers. Spike went back to the Teamsters union hall and begged them for a job. They found him a job in the warehouses at Walt Disney World, but before he could work there, he underwent an interrogation by one of the Teamsters veterans, a southern old-timer named John Brown. He wanted to know if Spike had a union background and why Spike wanted to join the Teamsters. Spike explained that he came from a family of Teamsters and aced the impromptu quiz. Not long after landing in the warehouses, Coskey was elected to be a shop steward. "It's because I have a big mouth," he said.

By this time, Spike was married and had a baby. He figured he would get paid a dollar more an hour to support his family if he were a truck driver, so he called a truck-driving company to learn how to drive a truck. It was a scam. He paid $3,000 to get his truck driver's license, but he did not learn a thing. He bid for a job to make truck deliveries at Disney World, but in order to do the job, he had to pass a test from the supervisor, a fireplug of a guy who Spike described as being mean as a snake. Spike and the supervisor had gotten into so many arguments so many times that Spike had lost count. Their mutual dislike was so great that when the supervisor's son started working at the warehouse and Spike introduced himself, the son said, "You're Spike? My dad hates you." Spike replied, "Good! The feeling is mutual."

Unfortunately for Spike, the supervisor also was the proctor for his truck-driving test. Spike recalls thinking, "I just wasted $3,000 and I'm never going to pass this test." The supervisor took him to the yard outside the distribution center for the test and gave him one of the tightest spaces, with pallets all around, for him to back the truck into. In the truck's cab, the supervisor growled, "Back it up." Spike thought, "There's no way this is going to work." Spike closed his eyes, slammed the truck into reverse, and prayed for the best. He drove the truck right into the spot. Other drivers who were watching the test jumped up on the side of the truck and shouted, "Goddamit! You're a truck driver now!"[3]

Over the next five years as a driver, Spike became active in Local 385. He first became a steward and then decided to run for a leadership position in 1999. He wasn't alone. Fresh off her stint as a temporary business representative, Donna-Lynne also had decided to run on a leadership slate, as did Clay Jeffries, who came from the UPS drivers' side of the union. The incumbent slate was headed by Ferenac and other backers of Ron Carey. Spike was on a pro-Hoffa slate led by Mike Stapleton, a longtime Local 385 leader who came from the truck-driving side of the union. Donna-Lynne joined a slate with Clay, headed by another longtime Local 385 leader, and it was the first time that they got to know each other. Clay had started at UPS off-loading packages at a warehouse in Cocoa, Florida, and became a driver and then a union steward. While she wasn't exactly impressed with him, Donna-Lynne didn't feel that he was a complete dolt. She sensed that Clay, red-haired and beer-bellied, was running for the position so he wouldn't have to be a UPS driver for the rest of his life. "Back then, I got along with him fine," she said. "My impression was he just wanted out of UPS."

In typical Teamsters fashion, Ferenac began an intimidation campaign against Spike, starting with a phone call to Spike's home right after Spike had decided to run on the competing leadership slate. On the call, Ferenac suggested it would be unwise for Spike to run against him. "I think it would be a mistake," Ferenac told him. "You're going to get slapped and you're going to get slapped hard." Spike was built like a football linebacker, but he admitted, "I'm not the toughest guy on the planet. But don't threaten me or I'll lose it." Spike told Ferenac, "Really? I'll be over there in 15 minutes, and I want you to point to the guy who is going to slap me." Spike hung up the phone, smashing the receiver.

A few days later, Ferenac came into the break room of the delivery warehouse at Disney World with a big-muscled guy. Ferenac was a loud talker and liked to take over any room he was in, and Spike interpreted their appearance as another effort to intimate him: here Ferenac was, trying to take over his break room. "If he doesn't intimate you, he tries to get someone else to intimate you." Spike said. "It's Teamsters politics."

Campaigning for a position at the local union was a second full-time job. Spike started his day job driving his rounds at 4 a.m. and worked until noon. Afterward, he camped out in the parking lots and break rooms around Disney World and UPS facilities, trying to talk to as many Teamsters members as possible. He would try to target the different groups of Teamsters workers at Disney—parking lot attendants, bus drivers, and costumed character performers. Often, when Spike was trying to talk to his members, managers at Disney World would attempt to escort him around the facilities, in clear violation of labor rules. Since the Disney warehouses sometimes received overseas containers, the resort was required to get a US Department of Homeland Security certification, and managers used that as an excuse to monitor Spike when he was on the property. When managers saw Spike, they would get on the radio and say, "Spike is in the building" and run out and ask what he was doing. Spike would tell the managers that he only was trying to make sure the contract was being followed. "We can stand here and fucking argue in front of my members all day and give them a little show, or let me do my job," Spike would tell them in proud Teamster fashion.

The pro-Hoffa slate led by Stapleton that included Spike won the election. But in an odd, Teamsters twist, both Donna-Lynne and Clay managed to join the Local 385 leadership team anyway, even though their slate lost. The treasurer on Stapleton's slate ended up being declared ineligible to run, through some manipulations by officials at the Teamsters Union now led by Hoffa. Because Clay had gotten the second-most votes for the position, he took over the job. Donna-Lynne also was asked to join the team. Before Ferenac left office, he had fired Donna-Lynne on Christmas Eve because she had refused to run with him, and she had filed charges against him with the Equal Employment Opportunity Commission (EEOC) over his refusal to pay her the same wages as a man. Knowing what a good job she had done, Stapleton hired her back as a business agent a week later, on New Year's Day, provided Donna-Lynne drop the EEOC charges. She did so but was not happy about it, since she felt she was owed money for the difference between what she was paid and what she ought to have been paid. When she was rehired, she got paid the same as the other men at Local 385.

Thus, Donna-Lynne, Clay, and Spike all started working as colleagues at Local 385 under Stapleton's leadership around the same time in 2000. Spike hated Clay from the very first time they met. One of the first things Clay did when getting to the Teamsters offices was to order Spike to move filing cabinets for him. "So, we got into it from Day One," Spike said.[4]

A couple of years later, Stapleton hired his daughter, Laura, to work as a bookkeeper at the union hall. Another Local 385 leader, Dave Concannon, also hired his daughter for an office job. They were mockingly dubbed "children of the regime" by their critics. But it was par for the course, since Teamsters locals all over the United States were notorious for their nepotism, with generations of Teamsters officials being the children of earlier Teamsters leaders.

"Union officials can act like royalty in ensuring that union leadership is passed to their children," writes Ashby. "Dynasties exist in monarchies—a prince or princess becomes king or queen when their parent, the ruling monarch, dies. Dynasties should not exist in democratic organizations."[5]

Laura Stapleton was about half Spike's age. They started talking to each other over long lunches, and no one at the union hall was any wiser when they secretly started dating. Soon, Laura and her girls had moved into a house with Spike, and Spike and Laura got engaged. He was now poor as a church mouse with many more mouths to feed.

Not long afterward, following confrontations with Clay and then with Stapleton, Spike was fired from Local 385. Spike had his suspicions that he had been set up, perhaps because he was dating the boss's daughter and Stapleton did not like it. But there were most likely other reasons. Spike felt he had an "X" on his back after he discovered that members wanting to leave Local 385 were not getting their calls returned by Clay. Spike also suspected that Clay was putting down the names of new Disney workers as having joined the union, in order to boost his recruiting targets, when they had done no such thing. Spike said when he raised the issue with Stapleton, the union boss told him, "Get out of my office."

"That, I think, honestly started the downfall for me," Spike said. Spike's firing was over something stupid. Stapleton had accidentally given him an extra week of vacation, and when the mistake was discovered, Spike had had to sacrifice another week of vacation the following year. But then Clay told Spike he had to give up yet another week, infuriating him. When Spike urged Laura to have her father intervene, she was told by Stapleton that it was up to Clay. Spike was having a meeting with his stewards in the union hall. He turned to them, before heading into Clay's office, and said, "Guys, if they're trying to screw me out of that vacation, this may be the last time I represent you as a business agent, because I'm going to lose my job."

Spike and Clay had started arguing in Clay's office about the vacation time when Stapleton walked in to find out what all the shouting was about. "Mike, if you're trying to steal a week's pay, then you both are going to have a problem," Spike said. Stapleton asked Spike if that was a threat, and Spike said it was a promise. Stapleton then fired Spike on the spot. Spike kicked a couple of trash cans walking out of the union hall.

Spike's firing required the approval of the executive board of the union local, and as a member of the leadership team, Donna-Lynne signed off on it, not fully realizing Spike's side of the story. Spike viewed it as "just deserts" from Donna-Lynne. "We had dated for ten years. We were no longer dating. I hook up with a girl half my age, the boss's daughter," Spike said.

Spike got banned not only from the local but also from the International Brotherhood of Teamsters. Not long afterward, Spike and Laura called off their engagement. It did not help that Spike had spent all day long complaining about her dad.

Unemployed and bitter at the Teamsters, Spike eventually fell in with an outfit aimed at keeping unions out of workplaces. Oftentimes, these consulting firms were staffed with former union officials who had been mistreated by their unions and decided to go over to "the dark side." Spike had heard about the job from his ex-wife, who told him that a former associate and her husband were working for the consulting firm. Spike asked her why she had never told him about it before he left the Teamsters. "You would have killed them both," she replied.

6

Clean Underwear

As a business agent for the character performers, as well as other central Florida workers, Donna-Lynne grew to have a dash of Cinderella's hope, Mulan's fearlessness, Anna's determination, and Snow White's talent for rallying a cast of animals to her side, or at least human performers dressed as animals. More than anything, Donna-Lynne acted as a fairy godmother to the character performers. Donna-Lynne saw her mission as protecting the magical kingdoms' most vital workers. If the Disney overlords made unfair demands of the character performers, she stood up for them. Her weapons were grievances, complaints to the National Labor Relations Board, and well-honed negotiating skills. Rather than spending time in the Teamsters' drab offices, Donna-Lynne preferred talking to performers backstage at Walt Disney World. She made sure that her "face" performers—the Disney World performers whose eyes were not hidden behind a costume—had the right makeup. She confirmed that her performers in Mickey Mouse and Goofy costumes had ice packs handy for when they were done with their sets. She checked that costumes were washed properly and not vectors of disease, as they had been in years past when performers complained of contracting pubic lice and scabies from improperly washed undergarments.

Though Donna-Lynne knew a lot when she took the job, she had furthered her education with several sessions courtesy of the Teamsters at the National Labor College outside Washington, DC. The college, at the time called the George Meany Center for Labor Studies, had opened in the late 1960s to train up-and-coming labor leaders. She took classes on business law, negotiations, and organizing.

One of Donna-Lynne's first victories as a business agent was winning the right to clean underwear for the character performers in 2001. Even though Carl Crosslin had campaigned against contaminated underwear when organizing the characters, performers still complained about getting pubic lice, rashes, ringworm, and scabies from the garments they wore underneath their costumes. The character performers also were still complaining about receiving undergarments that were stained and smelly. Disney officials had told the performers that company launderers were using hot water to clean the undergarments, but apparently that wasn't the case. "Things have been passed around," said Gary Steverson, a stilt walker who was a Teamsters steward. Before the changes pushed through by Donna-Lynne, the performers were required to hand in their undergarments along with the rest of their costumes before going home. They then picked up a different set the next day. With the changes Donna-Lynne negotiated, the performers were assigned individual undergarments and allowed to take them home and wash them themselves if they wished.[1]

It helped that Donna-Lynne knew firsthand that working as a costumed character could be a mixture of emotional rewards coupled with physical pain, and she put that knowledge to work now that she was a Teamster business agent for the costumed character performers. The daily hugs from children gave meaning to the performers' work. When they put a smile on the faces of sick children during their regular visits to a resort for the terminally ill, it was like being touched by an angel. The performers Donna-Lynne represented at Disney World viewed their positions more as missionaries of joy than as just punch-the-clock workers.

"Making people smile is my favorite part of my job. It's not just to entertain. People come here to escape the real world," said Steve Pollino, a longtime costumed character performer. "Disney entertainment—that brand is what brings people here to see us and we get to bring it to life. If it weren't for the character department, we would just be an amusement park. We get to bring to life everybody's favorite movies, everybody's favorite cartoons, all the Disney characters, whether it's classic Disney or Star Wars. That's our life. It's more than a job. Otherwise, I'd get a 9-to-5 job somewhere else."[2]

Some character performers, like Teresa Freeman, went to extraordinary lengths to get their jobs. Ever since she was a little girl, Freeman had wanted to make a living dancing in front of Cinderella's Castle. After college, she moved to Florida so she could work at Disney World. She started out in the costuming department because she was too heavy to be a character. She went to twelve auditions over two years before she lost enough weight to get a character performer job. "I had to lose more and more weight to dance on that castle stage," she said.[3]

Freeman believed the best part of her job was connecting with "the little guests." "You have to be truly empathetic," Freeman said. "You see the people around them and try to sense their relationships. For tons of children, we are a dream come to life. That carries a lot of responsibilities. We have to maintain the characters' integrity. It's different than driving a truck or working 9-to-5."

On the downside, the costumes were restrictive and could cause injuries when the performers were pushed or grabbed in the wrong way. The Mickey Mouse costume was heavy on the head. The awkward costume shoes often caused foot injuries. If one of the four theme parks at Disney World was producing a new show, Donna-Lynne tested it for safety. She donned the shoes worn by the performers and danced, slid, and ran across an empty stage to see if the floor surface tripped her. Safety concerns went beyond preventing performer falls. Not long after the opening of the "Fantasmic!" stage show, which showcased various Disney characters in a dream sequence, a sack worn by a performer playing John Smith, Pocahontas's love interest, caught fire from nearby pyrotechnics. The performer put out the fire while moving on an onstage barge without the audience knowing what was going on. Before the fiery accident, Donna-Lynne had argued with Disney managers over her concerns about the safety of flares onstage. The singeing of John Smith proved her point. The next day, performers on the show were instructed on where fire extinguishers were hidden onstage, and costumes were treated with flame retardant.[4]

Donna-Lynne insisted that coordinators who orchestrated the various parades in the four parks know how to drive the floats in case of an emergency in which the float driver could not drive. "You can't pull a float out of a jam if you don't know how it operates," Donna-Lynne insisted. While working in the parks, Donna-Lynne saw firsthand that if Cinderella's crown-shaped float was not budging, it could be worse than a lost glass slipper. Disney did not want to spend the money on new training, but Donna-Lynne negotiated it into the next contract.

These safety measures could be a matter of life or death. In 2004, Javier Cruz, a performer dressed as Pluto, was run over and killed when his foot got caught between two sections of a float and he lost his balance.[5] Disney was fined $6,300 by the Occupational Safety and Health Administration and the company implemented new safety rules for floats. "Once in a while you find that the company isn't just about money," Donna-Lynne said at that time. "It's rare."

As their union representative, Donna-Lynne felt like a momma bear protecting her cubs. "They're my kids," Donna-Lynne liked to say. "She's our mom," performers often said. Her "kids" were the highest profile workers at Disney World and part of the largest single-location workforce in the world. Disney World had close to seventy-seven thousand workers by the late 2010s. Over the years, Donna-Lynne had fought to include in the character performers' contracts the right to have a full hour to prep before they were required to go into the park in costume, and they had a half hour at the end of their shift to return their costumes or do other tasks.[6] Because of Donna-Lynne's efforts, warm-up time with coaches on hand to help the performers stretch was guaranteed, performers doing acrobatics were given special slip-proof shoes, and they all were given as much time out of costume as in costume during their shifts. Those performers who were "face characters" had a limit on their performance time outdoors of no more than an hour at a time, thanks to Donna-Lynne, who also made sure the performers were allowed at least two dress rehearsals before the curtain rose on a new show. Because of Donna-Lynne, the performers got paid time for dressing and walking to their stations.

Through the years, Donna-Lynne had gotten reinstated workers who had been accused of violating Disney's strict code of dress and conduct. Disney World's dress code traditionally had been detailed and often unyielding, the result of Walt Disney's desire for his employees to maintain a clean-cut image, though it evolved over the years.

"The Disney Look is a classic look that is clean, natural, polished and professional, and avoids 'cutting edge' trends or extreme styles," starts an early version of the "The Disney Look," the manifesto of dress and grooming standards that was given to every new theme park worker. "Often, it's the seemingly little things that detract from our Guests' enjoyment—chewing gum, having poor posture, using a cellular phone or frowning. Of course, smoking and eating onstage are also strictly prohibited."[7]

In the early years, workers were prohibited from wearing sunglasses if their eyes could not be seen, since dark lenses were "a block to interpersonal communication." They were encouraged to wear regular glasses in a "conservative" style. It went without saying that visible tattoos, body piercings, earlobe expansions, and skin implants were verboten, at least up until 2021. They either had to be covered up or temporarily removed while working. Deodorant was required, but perfume and cologne were prohibited. All workers had to wear underwear, and the underwear should not be visible beneath light-colored clothes. Fingernails could be painted but not in black, gold, silver, or any neon colors. Only one ring per hand was permitted, except for a wedding set, and only one earring in each ear was allowed. Facial hair on men was permitted, but it could not partially cover the face, like a soul patch. It had to be all fully grown in. "Extreme" hairstyles weren't tolerated, nor were "bi-level" hairstyles. Head shaving was permitted for men but not for women. Women could grow their fingernails no more than a quarter inch past their fingertips, and men had to keep their fingernails no longer than their fingertips.

If a performer needed to deviate from the "Disney Look" because of a character role, they needed to get permission from the company.[8] If an Orthodox Jew or a Sikh wanted to wear a headcover for religious reasons, they needed to make a request for an exception to the "Disney Look" with the company's employee relations department. Sometimes, the strictness of the company's standards flirted with legal action. Disney World once came under scrutiny after Gurdit Singh, a Sikh worker who wore a turban as an expression of his faith, called in the American Civil Liberties Union after claiming he was kept on an internal postal route that kept him out of public view. Under pressure, the company reversed course and allowed Singh to run routes visible to the theme park visitors. In another case that was eventually settled, Imane Boudlal sued Disney claiming she was prohibited from wearing a hijab as part of her Muslim faith while working at a Disneyland resort in California. Managers had told Boudlal it would ruin the Disney "look" and "negatively affect patrons' experiences" at the café where she worked in the hotel, the lawsuit said.[9]

The Disney Look loosened up through the years, with input from workers and Disney-visitor focus groups, who were shown photos of clothing and hairstyles and asked if they had objections to park employees wearing them. "We're not looking to be on the cutting edge, but we want to see what styles are becoming mainstream," said Melissa Valiquette, who was manager of costuming, cast image, and appearance at Walt Disney World.

In 1994, the rules were loosened even further to allow female workers to wear eye shadow and eyeliner, and balding male workers were permitted to wear toupees. In 2000, Disney allowed its park workers to grow mustaches in an effort to recruit more workers in a tight labor market. Three years later, male workers were allowed to wear braids, or cornrows provided they stayed above the collar, and female employees were allowed to wear hoop earrings. The Oxford shirts–only requirement was eased to allow turtleneck and mock turtleneck shirts.[10]

"Any additional leeway is a good thing," Donna-Lynne said at the time.

In spring 2021, in response to the social justice protests the previous year after George Floyd's death at the hands of police officers in Minneapolis, Disney became even more permissive in what it allowed. Disney started allowing workers to have visible tattoos, jewelry, long nails, and "gender-inclusive" haircuts. "The world is changing, and we will change with it, and continue to be a source of joy and inspiration for all the world," Josh D'Amaro, chair of Disney Parks, Experiences and Products, said. "We want our guests to see their own backgrounds and traditions reflected in stories, experiences and products they encounter in their interactions with Disney. And we want our cast members—and future cast members—to feel a sense of belonging at work."[11]

Donna-Lynne's good friend, Juleeann Jerkovich, a leader at the local United Food & Commercial Workers International Union, which also had workers at Disney, added, "As long as you can come to work, have a little more freedom and maintain the professionalism, I always think that's a great thing."[12]

Not everyone was on board with the changes. Some Disney fans felt Disney World should be a place where the outside world did not intrude on the fantasy. Longtime Disney World visitor Jonathan VanBoskerck wrote an opinion piece in the *Orlando Sentinel* that went viral on social media in 2021, criticizing Disney's newfound support for its workers' expressing themselves through their appearance.

"The problem is, I'm not traveling across the country and paying thousands of dollars to watch someone I do not know express themselves," VanBoskerck wrote. "I am there for the immersion and the fantasy, not the reality of a stranger's self-expression. I do not begrudge these people their individuality and I wish them well in their personal lives, but I do not get to express my individuality at my place of business."[13]

Donna-Lynne successfully pushed back when Disney tried to keep performers from disclosing to friends and relatives information about which characters they performed as, for fear it would break "the magic."[14] The company had told individual performers, "Cast members are expected to preserve the integrity of the Disney Character brand," according to a National Labor Relations Board complaint Donna-Lynne filed but later withdrew after a dispute was resolved. Donna-Lynne realized performers needed to share with future employers which characters they had played in order to get performing jobs elsewhere.

"They have family and friends that already know this and have pictures of themselves in their performing roles. It's out there," Donna-Lynne said at the time. "I believe in character integrity and not destroying the magic, but these are performers. A performer who plays Santa Claus and wants work, he goes out there and says, 'I played Santa Claus.'"

Disney was particularly sensitive about performers revealing which characters they played via social media, especially after a performer who worked as Aladdin's Princess Jasmine posted pictures of herself in costume, drunk, and drooling on an apartment building's balcony in the nearby Disney-built town of Celebration, Florida. Not only had she posted public images of herself drunk and in costume, but she had taken the costume off Walt Disney World property, which was forbidden. Poor Princess Jasmine lost her job. "I could not help her," Donna-Lynne said.

Donna-Lynne fought to put Jasmine and other workers on "rehire" status. When someone left the company, they were designated "rehire," "restricted rehire," and "no rehire." Because so many Disney performers would work several years at Disney World, leave, and then come back, being given a "rehire" status was just as important as other types of severance benefits. It left the door open for future employment, since that designation would stay in Disney's system forever—and not just at Disney World but other Disney-owned businesses too.

Given the thoroughness of the Disney code, it was not difficult for long-time costumed character performers to violate some part of it during their decades-long careers, and many would say that Donna-Lynne had saved them from getting fired at some point for various infractions. "Donna-Lynne was our department mom," said Pollino, a veteran costumed character worker. "She took care of everybody, everywhere, anywhere."[15]

Sometimes, Donna-Lynne had "frequent fliers," performers who needed her help to save their jobs after getting into trouble on several occasions. Usually, it was for the same infractions. They showed up to work late, had missing uniform pieces, or were insubordinate to managers. "When you clock in, you agree to the rules. If there is a safety issue, by all means, throw your hissy fit," Donna-Lynne said. "Anything else, obey now. File a grievance later."

One performer who played Goofy got into character too much. Employing method acting, he did things that he believed the character of Goofy would do, like pulling the legs out from under a performer playing Donald Duck. One time, a child tripped over them, and Donna-Lynne found her hands were tied. He had violated all four cardinal rules for Disney workers—safety, courtesy, show, and efficiency—and she could not help him.

Sometimes, Donna-Lynne did her job too well. She once had a male worker who was investigated by Disney management for sexually harassing a female employee. Donna-Lynne knew both workers. The woman was not one to make things up, and Donna-Lynne had witnessed the man acting inappropriately before. But Donna-Lynne had a job to do. She asked for witness statements, but the company investigators hadn't followed up by interviewing anybody. Like a good defense attorney, Donna-Lynne argued at a meeting with the male worker and Disney managers that the case should be dismissed since the company had not provided any independent witnesses to back up the allegations. The company relented and agreed to give the man his job back. After Disney officials left the room, the man came over and asked Donna-Lynne how she thought it went. He tried to pull her closer as she backed up against a wall. He grabbed her hand, but luckily, Donna-Lynne was able to escape out of the room. "Both sides have to uphold the contract," Donna-Lynne said. "The company didn't do its job."[16]

Disney maintained a point system when it came to disciplining wayward workers. A reprimand for an offense could earn a worker one or two points. Workers who had accumulated five points in a single year could be fired. Workers also could be terminated for arguing, being insulting or discourteous in front of a Disney guests, fighting, falsifying records, using or possessing drugs on the job, being convicted of a crime, violating operation rules that endangered guests or caused property damage, gambling or sleeping on the job, and continuing to violate the company's appearance guidelines.[17]

Donna-Lynne often walked through the dressing rooms to make sure the performers had everything they needed. Oftentimes, it was as simple as a burned-out lightbulb on a makeup mirror that needed to be replaced but had not been reported, each of the performers thinking someone else would take care of it. "We've gotten to the point where Disney knows what they're supposed to do," Donna-Lynne said. "They know I'm going to come out and check." When Donna-Lynne was a performer, most of the Disney managers came from the entertainment side of the business and knew what the performers needed. But sometime around the 2000s, after Donna-Lynne transitioned to the Teamsters, the managers started coming from other, non-entertainment sides of Disney's businesses, and Donna-Lynne saw her mission as educating them as to what their performers needed.

Donna-Lynne's favorite place to visit in her job as a Teamsters business agent was the Tri-Circle-D Ranch at Disney World, where the ponies for Cinderella's carriage and other animals for parades were kept. "They still had the original Disney concept—they're working hard together," she said.

"They're respectful, cheerful, love what they do. They didn't need anybody supervising them. Their job was to take care of those animals, just get them all dressed up and ready for parades."

When dealing with Disney managers who had conflicts with her performers, Donna-Lynne turned on the honey. But as a proud former Philadelphian, she was not afraid to use vinegar either. While walking around Disney World on inspections, she wore a badge slung around her neck that read "BA," identifying her as a union business agent. The performers joked that it really stood for "badass." But she was more of a problem-solver than a "badass." She believed that Teamsters often took a more confrontational approach because of their backgrounds in the transportation industry, which had a "fight the company" mentality. Donna-Lynne approached conflicts between performers and managers much more diplomatically than what she joked was the more typical Teamsters' approach of saying, "You screwed up! You need to fix this!" The first questions she would ask, in a slightly exasperated voice, were: "What's going on here? How did it get to this point? How do we fix it?" She always tried to have a solution on hand that she could present to the opposing Disney managers, who appreciated her experience and background as a performer. "It can't just be about fighting the company," she said. "You have to want to make things better for the employees and figure out how do you do that."

That philosophy was challenged by Disney's refusal to undo the firing of three "Festival of the Lion King" performers in 2014. The three Walt Disney World performers knew something was wrong when they touched their unitards before a show. Their undergarments were supposed to be freshly laundered but instead were damp with sweat and rainwater. Someone in the costuming department had moved the rack of sweaty costumes off the porch when it began raining and placed them inside the dressing room. The sweaty costumes had rubbed up against the performers' clean unitards hanging from racks.[18] With any other workforce, this might not be a big deal, but for Doug Bierderman, Drew Pearson, and Matthew Warfield, it was huge, since in years past performers had caught scabies and rashes after using costume pieces that were not thoroughly cleaned. The three "Festival of the Lion King" performers had a show in a few hours, and they did not want to put on the underwear. No unitards meant no show.

The costumes were elaborate for the "Festival of the Lion King," one of the most popular shows at Disney World. They had feathers and felt, animal prints, and fake fur that draped off the performers playing lions, elephants, zebras, and gazelles. The costumes were shared between two teams of performers who took turns dancing, singing, and doing acrobatics to wide-eyed audiences of parents, children, and Disney lovers of every age, every hour at the Animal Kingdom park at Disney World. During the show, acrobats flew through the air, and baton twirlers caught flaming bars in between displays of color, singing, and dancing.

When performers on one team were done with their show, they would hang their sweaty costumes out to dry on a rack located on a porch off the dressing room. In the dressing rooms were stretchable one-piece garments worn underneath the animal costumes. The performers were supposed to put on those clean undergarments for each hourly show. Bierderman, Pearson, and Warfield were performers in the "B" group. Bierderman, a beanpole of a guy who had studied interior design at Florida State University, was a leopard. Pearson, a Texas native with a boyish smile, played a warthog. Warfield, a tall, gregarious man from St. Louis, was an alligator.

All three had worked as performers at Disney World for years without any disciplinary problems; that is, until they refused to wear the undergarments, putting the evening show in jeopardy. One of the managers suggested spraying the undergarments with Febreze, but the performers would have none of it. After much back-and-forth with their managers, one of the managers asked, "Are you downing the show?" Warfield responded, "We don't have unitards and we don't know what to do." The next "Festival of the Lion King" show was canceled to the disappointment of almost one thousand Disney guests, many who had paid more than $100 each for a single-day entry into the theme park resort. Their manager told the performers, "You're troublemakers."

After the men were suspended and then fired for "conduct detrimental to the company," the first person they contacted was Donna-Lynne. As luck would have it, when the Lion King performers texted her after losing their jobs, Donna-Lynne was in contract negotiations on behalf of all character performers in a hotel conference room. The top Disney World labor relations managers were sitting at a table across from her. During a break, she pulled one of them aside, and asked, "What is going on? They did not have clean costumes."

The labor relations executive said, "Well, the manager made the decision . . ." Donna-Lynne cut him off and, uncharacteristically, got all Teamsters on him. "You need to fix this!" she said. "You can't do that. The costumes have to be clean and dry. The performers just stood by the contract."

The contract stated that all costumes "shall be clean and dry prior to each workday when given to a character performer and cleaned thereafter whenever necessary." If costumes were being shared, the contract required a minimum of twelve hours for cleaning and drying between uses and mandated that all shoes and head costumes be treated with disinfectant and dried. If performers were scheduled to be in the same character costumes for at least four days in a week, they would get assigned costumes that no one else could use.[19]

Donna-Lynne and the Disney labor relations manager had several conversations in the following days about the fired "Festival of the Lion King" performers. "You need to get them back to work," she told him. "They did nothing wrong." Donna-Lynne thought Disney had some nerve to fire the performers. Not long before the firings, a performer had found bed bugs in the men's dressing room of the "Festival of the Lion King" show. Before that, performers had gotten skin reactions from new unitards. Donna-Lynne herself had once caught ringworms wearing unclean tights when she was performing as a member of Aladdin's harem. "It's ridiculous to treat good performers like this," Donna-Lynne said.

When the cajoling did not work, Donna-Lynne took it to the next level and filed a grievance against Disney World on behalf of the three "Festival of the Lion King" performers. Union members liked it when Donna-Lynne filed grievances, because it gave them a sense that the union was doing what their dues were paying it to do: defend them, represent them, give them a voice, and not make them feel like they were being pushed around by the largest entertainment company in the world. Grievances were not cheap. Between the lawyers, costs of a venue, the arbitrator, and administrative costs, filing a grievance could cost Disney and the union several thousand dollars per side. Sometimes workers facing grievance hearings brought along their ministers or parents, not realizing that it was not like a trial where character witnesses could bolster their cases.

The grievance process started with a meeting between Donna-Lynne, a labor relations manager from Disney, and a Disney entertainment general manager. After talking over the case, they could not resolve the dispute, so the case went to a joint standing committee made up of a Disney executive and a representative from the Service Trades Council Union, the coalition of unions including the Teamsters that represented unionized service workers at Disney World. The two members on the committee were split when they heard the case, so it went to arbitration. Before an independent arbitrator, Disney officials argued that the Lion King performers had been dishonest in describing the unitards as soiled and that they had violated the contract by creating a work stoppage. Donna-Lynne argued that the unitards had been contaminated and that the performers were unjustly fired. She demanded they get their jobs back with full benefits and seniority.[20]

The arbitrator sided with Donna-Lynne and ordered Disney World to rehire Bierderman, Pearson, and Warfield with back pay and their seniority and full benefits restored. "Since the unitards on the racks in question were not clean and dry, the grievants were not required to wear them," the arbitrator wrote.

"Once upon a time, Cinderella was forced to work grueling hours without pay for her evil stepmother," said an article in a Teamster newsletter about the decision. "Today, she is protected from unfair management courtesy of a strong union contract negotiated by the Teamsters."

While the performers were fighting to get their Disney jobs back, they had taken part-time jobs at rival Universal Orlando Resort, a nonunionized shop, and worked in local theater to make ends meet. All three performers came back to Disney World. The performers were deeply grateful to Donna-Lynne for getting their jobs back. "From the very beginning she had our backs and always kept our best interests in mind," Warfield said. "She took on our grievance with fire and drive and never gave up."[21]

7

Disney Labor

How Disney World grew to have the nation's largest single-site workforce and one of the largest number of workers covered by union contracts in the United States is a tale worthy of a Disney story itself. In the late 1950s, Walt Disney hired a consultant to tell him where the best location would be for an East Coast theme park. His first theme park, Disneyland, in Anaheim, California, had been a wild success after it opened in 1955. Walt Disney wanted a location that could attract visitors from the East Coast and the Midwest. Buzz Price, a consultant, picked Florida but around Palm Beach in the southern part of the state. Walt Disney feared a location too close to the beach would be a distraction and also make the park vulnerable to hurricanes. A later survey conducted by the company picked Ocala, Florida, about eighty miles north of Orlando, as the top spot, with Orlando coming in second.[1]

Highways were ultimately what attracted Walt Disney to the Orlando area.[2] Interstate 4, which now bisects metro Orlando, was being constructed in the early 1960s. The interstate eventually connected to the Florida Turnpike in the Orlando area. It joined Interstate 95 around Daytona Beach to the east and Interstate 75 to the west near Tampa. The Florida Turnpike bisected the state north-to-south, while Interstate 75 led all the way through the Upper Midwest. Interstate 95 connected the entire Eastern Seaboard, from Florida to Maine. Both highways connected to Interstate 10, the southernmost cross-country highway, stretching from Florida to California. So, residents of any state in the mainland United States could get to a new Disney park in Florida through the US interstate highway system. Plus, Walt Disney had family ties to the area. Early in their lives together, Walt Disney's parents had lived in central Florida, just dozens of miles from where the theme park resort would be built.

The eventual Florida theme park was built on more than 27,000 acres of swampy wilderness filled with wild hogs, turkeys, and deer in Orange and

Osceola Counties. It was secretly purchased parcel by parcel across almost fifty transactions for $5 million, using fake names and shell companies. Walt Disney had wanted to err on the side of having too much land to hold his dreams for the "Florida Project." After Disneyland opened in the mid-1950s, businesses had snapped up land around the California theme park, allowing little room for it to grow. The Florida Project, conceived a decade later, was kept secret so that land speculators would not drive up the price of parcels. The company set up dummy companies with names like "Latin American Development and Management Corp." and "Reedy Creek Ranch Corp." in Miami to purchase the land, using real estate agents who did not know the identity of their client. Most of the land transactions, some for as little as $100 an acre, were handled in cash to avoid a paper trail.[3]

Residents in Orlando knew someone was making massive land purchases, but they did not know who. It became a great guessing game as to who was behind the giant land grab. The land purchaser remained a mystery until an *Orlando Sentinel* reporter, a "girl reporter" as her own newspaper referred to her, got on the case. Emily Bavar, who was actually a forty-five-year-old woman, figured it out and, on a hunch, directly posed the question in 1965 to Walt Disney during a media junket celebrating the ten-year anniversary of Disneyland in California. The cat was out of the bag.[4]

Tourists had been coming to the Sunshine State for decades, including many former soldiers who first came to Florida for training during World War II. Many of those soldiers returned to live in Florida after the war, and others came back for vacations with their families, visiting old tourism warhorses such as Cypress Gardens in Winter Haven, Bok Tower Gardens in Lake Wales, Busch Gardens Tampa Bay, and the glass-bottom boats of Silver Springs in Ocala. In Orange County—where most of Disney World would be constructed—citrus and cattle dominated the area formerly called Mosquito County. Before Disney World's arrival, Martin Marietta was the largest employer, and the area was overshadowed by the Space Coast to the east, where the nation's first manned rocket launches were lifting off from Cape Canaveral.

There was no guarantee that Disney World was going to be a success. Walt Disney died only a year after announcing the plans for the "East Coast Disneyland," so the job of shepherding the project fell to his brother, Roy Disney, who would die almost three months after the theme park resort opened in 1971.

Disney's first big labor agreement in Florida was with the workers who built the Magic Kingdom and the two resorts that initially made up Walt

Disney World. But that agreement came only when initial worker strife during the construction of Magic Kingdom led in the late 1960s to the biggest labor strike in central Florida's history. Its resolution laid the groundwork for decades of relative labor peace between Disney and its unions. The strike started in 1968 when Elmer Sevor, a business manager for Operating Engineers Local 673, started organizing sixty employees working for a contractor doing excavation work. The workers voted to strike for recognition of the union and the equivalent union-scale wages. After episodes of rock-throwing and tire-slashing, former governor Claude Kirk ordered sheriff's departments from Orange and Osceola Counties to maintain peace on the picket lines around the Disney property. Kirk did not want any literal, or metaphorical, roadblocks to building what would be one of the biggest economic engines in the state, and he sent an emissary to monitor the strike with an open landline to the governor's office. At one point, a platoon of officers and deputies pushed picketing workers away from the fence at the Disney property line inch by inch.[5]

When negotiations eventually broke down, thousands of construction workers in central Florida, from Orlando to the Space Coast, conducted a one-day strike that culminated with a rally at the Citrus Bowl in Orlando. Construction projects across the state went idle. Soon, Disney agreed to use union workers and settled the month-long strike. National leaders of the AFL-CIO unions and Disney officials negotiated a three-year contract that was then ratified by the local unions. The contract pledged that there would be no strikes or work slowdowns, and the unions were promised that hiring would be done through local union hiring halls.[6]

While construction workers labored in the late 1960s to build the East Coast park, Disney picked fourteen local young women to be the first employees to engage with the public. These fourteen women, hired mainly based on their looks, wore miniskirts and manned a preview center at the intersection of Interstate 4 and State Road 535, starting in 1970 and told guests what to expect from the theme park. Over 1 million people visited the preview center in the year leading up to Disney World's opening in October 1971, and occasionally a costumed performer would show up dressed as a beloved Disney character.[7] "Help Wanted: But Only Pretty Girls with Happy, Friendly Spirits," read a headline in the *Orlando Sentinel* for an unsurprisingly sexist article about the preview center women. "Girls must be at least 18 years of age, attractive and should enjoy meeting and being with people," the article said.[8] Held up as an exemplar of that Disney spirit was an early hire named Debbie Dane, who met with governors and mayors as a Disney World "ambassador." She was described in a 1971 Disney press release as typifying "the happy, friendly spirit of her fellow employees—the kind of qualities that are sought in young women now applying at the Walt Disney World Employment Center."[9]

Despite the sexism apparent in the job requirements for being an "ambassador," a recruiting brochure from 1969 struck an inclusive note, informing prospective employees that Disney frowned on cliques and stating, "We accept people as they are." "If people are 'with us' in our goal, we accept them as they are . . . short, tall . . . any race . . . any religion . . . any political persuasion or any accent," the brochure said.[10] Workers were encouraged to get relatives or friends to apply for jobs. Disney posted help wanted ads in the *Orlando Sentinel,* and potential employees had to go through as many as four rounds of interviews in trailers on the Magic Kingdom grounds with Disney managers from California before they were hired.

"You are now a part of the most exciting event in the history of Walt Disney Productions," the then Walt Disney president Donn Tatum wrote to new employees. "We have our own traditions . . . our own Disney ways for working together."[11]

A script that accompanied a training manual urged the new Disney workers to "be aggressively friendly." "Greet guests first and genuinely smile," the script said. "Look directly at guests and be observant. A personal comment on clothing camera equipment, children, etc. can make a guest feel recognized as an individual."[12]

George Kalogridis, who would go on to be president of both Walt Disney World in Florida and Disneyland in California, was first hired as a busser in 1971. After graduating from high school, he had gone to a modular home on recently cleared Florida scrub land to apply for a job at the theme park resort that would open shortly. He was called into the house in a group of ten other applicants and told that whichever room he walked into would determine where he worked at Disney World. There were rooms for hotel workers, food workers, and ride operators.

"Each one was hiring for something different," said Kalogridis. "I could have gone one door, either way, and my life would have been different."[13]

With a deadline looming and concerns rising that the Magic Kingdom would not be finished in time for the opening, Disney took over the construction from the contractor and devoted all its resources to finishing the project. As workers were hired, construction continued almost night and day to get the park ready for the opening, and almost every hour something new seemed to pop up out of nowhere in the park. Preparations continued up until opening day, with workers laying sod at the Contemporary Resort just hours before VIPs and reporters arrived to tour the Magic Kingdom.

"It was like an army of ants," said Forrest Bahruth, who was hired in January 1971 as a show director responsible for staging and choreographing parades and shows. "Everything was under construction. Interiors were still being put in. Roofing was still being put on top. There was painting, landscaping. Things were arriving by the moment. It was like trucks going everywhere."[14]

On opening day, Disney had six thousand workers on hand. "It was like another world. You had never seen anything like the characters, the architecture and the buildings," said Barbara Maxwell, who was hired two months before the Magic Kingdom opened. "You really wanted to spend time walking around and looking, but there was always a line."[15]

Two things have stuck in the memories of the longtime employees from that opening day. The first was "The Photo"—an image of thousands of Disney World workers standing in front of Cinderella's Castle with Mickey Mouse and other costumed characters holding hands in front. Two weeks later, it was featured on the cover of *Life* magazine.

"They brought all the characters up, staged them first, and then they tried to keep all the different workers together based on the colors of their costumes," said Chuck Milam, who was one of Disney World's first hires, after getting a tip about a job opening from a transplanted Disney executive whose new house he was landscaping. "If you were in Fantasyland and in yellow, you would go over there."[16]

The second was the parade. It featured a 1,076-member marching band conducted by Meredith Willson, the composer of the Broadway show *The Music Man*. There were four thousand Disney entertainers marching through the theme park, a mass choir, and trumpeters from the US Army Band. Hundreds of birds were released into the air along with thousands of, less environmentally friendly, multicolored balloons. "It was the biggest thing I had ever seen," Bahruth said.

Around ten thousand visitors showed up on that first day, which at today's much larger Walt Disney World would represent about ninety minutes' worth of visitors entering.[17] By 2020, on any given day, Walt Disney World had the population of a small city. The resort could host as many as 350,000 people at one time. These crowds included up to 150,000 visitors to the parks, more than 140,000 overnight guests staying at hotels, and more than 61,000 workers. There also were around fifty permanent residents, mostly employees, who lived in manufactured homes on the resort's property.[18]

It wouldn't be until Thanksgiving 1971, almost three months after opening day, that Disney executives had an answer about whether the new resort was a success; that's when cars trying to get into the Magic Kingdom stretched for miles down the interstate. "It was very clear after that first Thanksgiving that the public definitely liked what we were doing," Kalogridis said. "That first Thanksgiving, that was the moment."

As part of the contract agreements following the strike in 1968, the construction unions had promised there would be no strikes or work disruptions. The deal with the construction workers paved the way for later agreements with the service workers under the umbrella of the Service Trades Council Union. The service workers who were covered by the Service Trades Council Union contract interacted with visitors and provided tourists with the Disney experience. But it wasn't always easy.

"This is a very difficult company to work for in terms of regimentation," said Harvey Totzke, a longtime head of the Service Trades Council Union in the 1990s and 2000s. "As part of their uniform, they have to wear a permanent smile, even on days when the last thing they want to do is smile."[19]

Disney executives had a more benign, if not oblivious, view of labor relations. Each Disney worker "is trained to treat each and every Guest with the utmost care and respect. And they do this consistently because they are treated exactly the same way by the Disney leadership: with the utmost care and respect," writes former Disney World executive vice president of operations Lee Cockerell in his book *Creating Magic,* with no trace of irony.[20]

In its latest incarnation, the Service Trades Council Union was made up of local unions from the International Alliance of Theatrical Stage Employees, the United Food and Commercial Workers, two locals from Unite Here, the Transportation Communications Union, and the Teamsters. Collectively, the six union locals represented a range of workers that included singers, actors, food servers, lifeguards, custodians, housekeepers, hotel workers, bus drivers, chefs, fishing guides, monorail drivers, makeup artists, garment cutters, garbage haulers, launderers, ride operators, bartenders, and park greeters. The contracts they negotiated prior to the coronavirus pandemic covered more than half of the seventy-seven thousand workers at Disney World.

Disney recognized the Service Trades Council Union as the exclusive collective bargaining representative for Disney World service workers in April

1972, seven months after the park opened, when a majority of employees signed cards saying they wanted to be part of a union. Under the council's constitution, all collective bargaining agreements would be approved by a majority of the council, and the first agreement was approved in June 1972. However, one of the unions put the unity of the young council to the test by refusing to execute the agreement since its members had failed to approve it. Local 855 of the International Alliance of Theatrical Stage Employees (IATSE) and Moving Picture Machine Operators of the United States and Canada argued that they were under no legal obligation to honor the agreement, since its members had voted it down. Disney World challenged that interpretation, and a panel of National Labor Relations Board judges agreed with Disney officials, saying the IATSE local was engaging in unfair labor practices. The judges ordered the local to follow the agreement.[21]

The union presence at Disney World was unique to the tourism hub of Orlando, since Florida was a right-to-work state, meaning workers could enjoy the benefits of a union contract without being compelled to pay dues to the unions that negotiated them. Universal Orlando Resort, Disney World's main competitor in Florida, managed to stave off repeated efforts to unionize its workforce since its opening in 1990. The last effort in 1999—a push by the Actors' Equity Association to unionize three hundred performers—attracted well-known TV actors Jean Stapleton, Tony Randall, and Jack Klugman to the cause. But Universal fought back hard. The company required performers to attend paid meetings where Universal executives lectured them on the disadvantages of joining a union. And the night before the union vote, Universal held its annual awards banquet where the company honored singers, dancers, actors, and stuntpeople while providing an open bar.

"Working for Universal isn't a bad thing. We're not talking about some evil ogre," said Doug Truelsen, a Universal Studios actor who was on the organizing committee for the union at the time. "We just want guarantees of things they say we have."[22]

The Universal organizing effort failed.

At Disney World, the unions could send letters to new workers asking to meet with them if they were interested in joining. If a new worker was interested, a union representative would set up a meeting somewhere at Disney World on company time but out of view of guests. The unions and Disney also set up joint labor/management committees with the goal of having open lines of communications that could diffuse or resolve any disputes.

As a result, after the construction workers' strike in the late 1960s, there were only a handful of other strikes at Disney World in Florida, and these were small in size and didn't last long. In 1980, musicians who performed all live music at the resort's parks and nightclubs were unhappy with their wages. The musicians' strike in October 1980 lasted only eight days, but it was given a jolt when 750 construction workers building Disney World's second theme park, Epcot, walked off their jobs in sympathy.[23] It took place during one of the greatest times of union activism in Orlando's tourism industry, at least since the mass one-day strike in the late 1960s that led to the first labor agreement at Disney World. During the same week that workers halted construction at Epcot, workers building a new terminal at Orlando International Airport also walked off their jobs. The airport walkout had been motivated by a contractor's refusal to engage in collective bargaining. Several workers were injured on the picket line when a truck drove through the picketers at the entrance to the construction site in a rare instance of union violence in Orlando. The idled airport workers joined the musicians in picketing outside Disney World that week.

The musicians' strike forced the cancelation of live music at Disney World for more than a week, and several touring acts backed out of performing to honor the picket line. Disney sued the musicians' union, the American Federation of Musicians Local 398, claiming it had fostered a secondary boycott when the Epcot construction workers walked off the job in solidarity, but the lawsuit was dropped after the musicians agreed to go back to work. The musicians got a pay increase of more than 8 percent, as well as bonuses.[24]

Two other strikes occurred on Disney World property but were directed at third-party companies that ran businesses at the resort. Workers at the Grosvenor Resort at Walt Disney World went on strike in September 1996 over unfair labor practices and were subsequently fired. The National Labor Relations Board later ruled that the resort owed the workers back pay even though most had found other jobs. In May 2002, almost four hundred Teamsters-affiliated workers at the Swan and Dolphin hotels went on strike and picketed in front of the resort after rejecting a three-year contract. Although the hotels were on Disney property, they were owned by Tishman Hotel Corp. The hotel workers ended the strike two weeks later after approving a contract that made it easier to file grievances when workers didn't get a forty-hour work week. "The workers feel their backs are to the wall," Stapleton, head of the local Teamster affiliate, said at the time.[25]

It was a different story for Disney's California parks, where workers carried out a major strike in 1984 that marked a hardening of Disney's views on labor. Nearly two thousand workers carried out the largest strike in Disney's history, one that lasted twenty-two days, after Disney proposed a two-year wage freeze, no health insurance for part-time workers, and the outsourcing of some jobs during contract talks. The workers overwhelmingly rejected the offer and created picket lines around Disneyland, calling it "The Friendliest Strike on Earth," in a playful twist on Disneyland's moniker as "The Happiest Place on Earth." The workers waved banners that said, "Please go to Knott's Berry Farm today, thank you," a reference to a crosstown competitor, and held a candlelight vigil outside the park. Picketers sneaked into the park, where they passed out pro-union pamphlets. Disney responded by going to court to get a temporary picket ban. Scores of workers protested outside Disneyland in defiance of the ban, and half a dozen union leaders were arrested after they refused to leave. A short time later, the California Supreme Court lifted the picketing ban, and workers responded by going to the park to tear up letters from the then Disneyland president Dick Nunis, who warned the striking employees they would be replaced if they did not return to work by midweek.[26] This was the same Dick Nunis who in a 1972 Disney World employee manual had told workers, "It takes a happy crew to produce a happy show."[27]

Disney employees were surprised by the hardball response and believed it marked a watershed change in labor relations at the parks in California and Florida, away from how the company had operated under founder Walt Disney. For Disney employees, the 1984 strike seemed to mark the end of a paternalistic relationship between Disney and its theme park workers who had shouted on the picket line, "Bring back Walt!" The ironic part of that battle cry was that Walt Disney's first brush with workers' attempts at labor organizing had not gone well. In 1941, animation artists at Walt Disney Productions tried to unionize in an effort that was led by star animator Art Babbitt, who was an integral part of Walt Disney's creative team. Feeling betrayed, Walt Disney fired Babbitt and other animators who had joined the Screen Cartoonist's Guild. In response, more than three hundred members of the studio's staff went on strike for nine weeks, in the middle of production on the films *Dumbo* and *Bambi,* and picketed with signs that read, "Are We Mice or Men?" After federal arbiters were called in for an arbitration hearing, Disney offered the strikers a union contract, which was accepted.[28]

After the Disneyland strike in 1984, theme park workers in Florida and California felt there was a hardening of Disney's views on labor relations, and there was no longer an assumption that the company was going to have the workers' best interests in mind when making decisions. The unions and labor managers at Disneyland eventually returned to the negotiating table after word got back to Disney officials that the striking workers planned to protest outside Nunis's home. The California workers later approved a new contract in which they got two of the three things they had demanded— keeping health insurance for part-time workers and limits on outsourcing. But bad blood remained between the striking workers and those who had crossed the picket line, and many workers left the company.

Back in Florida, Disney World's unionized workers never had a work stoppage on the scale of the 1984 strike in California, but the service workers flirted with striking several times, especially as Disney, beginning in the 1980s and after fighting off two corporate takeover battles, started offering cash bonuses instead of wage raises during contract negotiations.

"We're dealing with a new entity," Totzke, the Service Trades Council Union leader said at a news conference during contract talks in 1985. "We have not encountered a Disney this tough before."[29] In many ways, the contract talks between Disney and the Service Trades Council Union reached a turning point in 1985 when the union coalition representing about half of the Disney workforce agreed to cash bonuses that ranged from $300 to $1,600 in lieu of a change to the pay-scale during the first two years of the contract, as well as a 4 percent wage hike in the contract's third year. "Disney now helps keep wages around here low," John Hinson, a carpenter at Disney, told the *Orlando Sentinel* at the time.[30]

The Disney workers weren't alone, though, in losing ground on wage increases during contract negotiations in the 1980s.[31] "By the mid-1980s, concessionary bargaining had spread to virtually every organized industry— from auto, steel, and rubber production workers, to service employees in Las Vegas hotels, state hospitals and city services," writes Kim Moody in *An Injury to All.* "Along with a number of important and usually well-noted changes in the US economy and workforce, the decay of union power has contributed to the first major, long-term decline in the standard of living of the American working class as a whole to occur in the twentieth century."

During labor talks in 1988, 1991, and 2001, the possibility of strikes hung over contract talks between Disney and the Service Trades Council Union in Florida, and federal mediators were called in. But those negotiations eventually reached agreements. In 1988, after unionized workers had rejected a contract proposal, Nunis, now in Florida, sent a letter to workers warning them they could be replaced and lose all their benefits if they walked off the job. A vote on the contract had to be canceled after several workers were discovered to have voted more than once. Another vote was scheduled, and the contract was approved by the workers, a decision that reflected the reality that only about half of the workers covered by the contract were union members, thanks to Florida's status as a right-to-work state.[32] "The morale here is pretty low," Rex Berkebile told the *Orlando Sentinel*.[33]

Many union employees also said they likely would not have honored a strike line anyway.[34] Overall, that was true of other industries across the United States. "The reluctance to strike was no doubt reinforced by the fact that most serious strikes ended with concessions anyway, and a few ended in serious defeat," Moody said about that era in the 1980s.[35]

A federal mediator was called in for the 1991 negotiations after wages became a sticking point, as well as some workers' inability to get a forty-hour work week from the company, but an agreement was eventually reached. In some ways, a consolidation of operations within management also contributed to the company's changed, hardball attitude toward its workers. In the 1990s, the parks division and resort division at Disney World were streamlined to create a centralized management structure. As a result, managers who had been working at hotels were now at theme park operations. "Instead of separate domains with fuzzy boundaries, we had a clear structure that enabled us to make faster decisions, manage costs more efficiently, streamline our process and procedures, communicate more effectively, and better utilize capital resources," Cockerell said.[36]

Some of the changes got Disney caught up in a National Labor Relations Board charge in the mid-1990s that it was trying to farm out Teamsters and Equity performers to work in shows run by Disney affiliates in an effort to avoid having to be covered by the union contract. Equity officials had demanded documents about the affiliates, wanting to show that they were part of Walt Disney World in Florida and should be covered by the contract, but Disney didn't provide them all. The National Labor Relations Board called Disney's response to the union "a sham" and ordered Disney to provide the information and make sure performers rights weren't being undermined.[37]

Two decades later, in 2017, the US Department of Labor reached a settlement in which Disney agreed to pay $3.8 million in back pay to more than sixteen thousand theme park workers in Florida who had been charged fees for the maintenance of their costumes. The extra fees, in some cases, pushed the workers' wages below the federal minimum. The agency also said Disney wasn't paying their workers for pre-shift and post-shift work. The Department of Labor was using Disney as an example to other companies. "These violations are not uncommon and are found in other industries as well," said Daniel White, a Department of Labor official.[38]

8

Fifteen Dollars an Hour or Bust

The Service Trades Council Union and Disney were negotiating a new contract in late summer 2017. The contract talks were among the most important in years for the coalition of unions. A majority of the leaders who made up the coalition were pushing for a fifteen dollars an hour starting minimum wage, something once unthinkable for Disney workers. Over a period of three years, the proposed raise would represent a 50 percent increase from the current ten dollars an hour starting minimum wage.

The leaders of the Service Trades Council Union were divided on whether demanding a starting hourly wage of fifteen dollars was a realistic request. Some worried they were giving up better health-care insurance and pension benefits in exchange for higher wages. The heads of the three largest union affiliates in the coalition—two Unite Here locals and the Teamsters Local 385—were confident they would succeed with their demand of fifteen dollars an hour. The heads of the other unions thought such a wage hike was a pipe dream and Disney would never accept it. Some thought that it was being pushed by the three locals because their leaders were up for reelection that year and they wanted to give members a reason to vote for them. Plus, Disney was dangling a $1,000 bonus over the heads of workers if they signed the contract, and the workers were not going to get the bonuses without an agreement being approved.

"Internally, Disney knows the council is fighting against itself," said Ed Chambers, who led the coalition of unions at the time and was head of the United Food & Commercial Workers local. "We have people who would like to have that raise. Today, we gave them 12,000 signatures on a petition saying, 'We don't want your stinking bonus.' But $1,000 is a lot of money. We all want more money . . . but we have no exit strategy."[1]

Disney World was one of the largest private-sector unionized workforces left in the United States, but some Disney workers at the bottom rung of the wage scale had trouble making ends meet. They squeezed in with four or five other people in two-bedroom apartments. Others slept in run-down motels along a tourist strip not far from the theme park resort. Some made hour-long commutes to live in cheaper neighborhoods on the edges of metro Orlando. Many workers had to choose each week among paying for food, gas, rent, or medicine.[2]

The coalition of union locals was a heterogeneous bunch, and each union had its own personality and culture. Besides the character performers, Teamsters Local 385 also represented rental car workers, UPS drivers, and hotel employees. During union business, members referred to each other as "brother" or "sister" and, whether through reputation or history, the union carried an old-school swagger about it. Teamsters Local 385, along with two Unite Here locals, 737 and 362, dominated the coalition in numbers and money. The Unite Here locals represented lower wage, worker-bee employees at Disney World: food and beverage workers, housekeepers, park greeters, and ticket takers. The United Food & Commercial Workers Local 1625 represented salesclerks and merchandising workers. They liked flexibility in their work schedules, and they did not necessarily want to work forty hours a week. The International Alliance of Theatrical Stage Employees Local 631 represented the stagehands and technicians who worked on Disney World's many shows, and they came from creative, theatrical backgrounds. The workers at the Transportation Communications Union Lodge 1908 were on the move: they drove boats and monorails, but some also worked as bellhops and front desk clerks.

The three smaller unions could be steamrolled by member numbers if they did not go along with what the Teamsters and two Unite Here locals wanted, and that was what was going on with the negotiations for a new contract. The Teamsters and Unite Here leaders were urging members to hold out for the minimum fifteen dollars an hour. Disney negotiators were proposing to give workers a fifty-cent increase each year for the next several years, and they were using as leverage the $1,000 bonus per worker that they already had given to Disney workers in California. The bonus was granted after former president Donald Trump signed tax cut legislation in 2017. Disney would not distribute the bonuses in Florida until the Disney World workers reached an agreement on the wage negotiations. "Our side is absolutely right, $10 an hour, and you're not doing very well. You are poor. But $10.50 an hour is $20 a week better than what you were earning," Chambers said.[3]

Union workers had tried to grab Disney's attention with a series of protests outside the Walt Disney World resort and elsewhere. Chambers, who was trying to hold the coalition together, had come close to getting Disney to pay the $1,000 bonus without a contract signed, but then Unite Here workers protested outside Disney's shareholders meeting in Houston, in an attempt to embarrass the company, and the Disney negotiators dropped the idea. Chambers, who was older by a few decades than the other union leaders, had been doing contract negotiations for more than thirty years. At one time, when he was a young man, Chambers had been the grenade-thrower among the union negotiators, pushing hard for better benefits and wages by performing stunts. One of his favorite stunts involved posting thousands of bumper stickers that read "Bucks not Bonuses" all over Disney World when the company wanted to offer a bonus instead of a wage increase. But now, Chambers regarded himself as the wizened adult in the room.

"If all the leaders from the six unions come out here and trash the company, who is the company going to go to, to get a deal?" Chambers said privately at one of the protests the unions held during negotiations. He had gone to the protest more out of solidarity than from any belief that the protests were having any impact. "Somebody has to stay out of this mess," he said.

Not surprisingly, what Disney officials feared more than anything were work stoppages. The lack of strikes by the workers at Disney World, except in the very beginning in 1968, were part of a nationwide trend of declining work stoppages in the last decades of the twentieth century. Several strikes, most noticeably the federal air traffic controllers' failed walk off the job in 1981, had been executed with diminishing success in the last decades of the twentieth century and the first decades of the twenty-first, as employees learned to bring in replacement hires. While it also may be that labor unions and companies had become better at reading each other over the decades, the likely explanation was that unions had lost a lot of their leverage.[4]

Union negotiations with Disney had become trickier over the decades too, counterintuitively, as they had become more transparent. Back in the 1980s, the union representatives and the Disney negotiators would lock themselves in a room until a deal was reached. By the start of the 2000s, the negotiations took place in semipublic with dozens of workers invited into the hotel room ballroom to observe the talks. Plus, the Disney negotiators seemed to care about money more. In decades past, it was more about relationships. "When you have 60 to 80 people in the room, you can't be as frank. You have to pick and choose your words, which means it takes longer to get to the bottom line. That's a bit more difficult," Chambers said.[5]

In 2018, as the multi-month negotiations for a new contract with the Service Trades Council Union were heating up, the then Disney CEO Robert Iger earned $65 million while leading the California-based entertainment company—about one thousand times the median salary of all Disney employees.[6]

The differential felt staggering to the union negotiators. "You take Iger. I don't know the guy. I'm not trashing the guy. But his bonus? That would be life-changing for these guys. You take $5 million out of that? And that's life-changing for these guys. It's hard for us hourly folks to relate to that," Chambers said. "Everybody out here deserves more. It's a hard pill to swallow when you see how much the folks in California are making."

At a rally outside Disney World in February 2018, Eric Clinton, who headed one of the two large Unite Here locals in Orlando, said the $10.71 an hour that was the average wage at Disney World was unacceptable. He lambasted the $1,000 bonus offered by Disney as a trade-off for accepting lower wages. "Disney said we will give you $1,000 if you agree to stay poor," Clinton said. "Let us be clear. Disney cast member deserve a living wage. We will not allow a $1,000 trick of a bonus to be held over our heads. We're here to negotiate wages, not bonuses."

R. J. Green, a food service worker at Magic Kingdom, believed Disney would not have been offering the $1,000 a worker bonuses if not for the corporate tax breaks a Republican-controlled Congress had enacted in the previous year while some Disney workers were living at poverty level by working to make Orlando the nation's No. 1 tourist destination. "There are two monsters we are battling—wage negotiations and a path out of poverty, and they go hand in hand," Green said. "The company thinks it can trick us into taking this $1,000. Their bonus is a short-term solution to a long-term problem. We make magic for families every single day, and there's no reason we should not be able to provide for our families when we have to work 14-hour days to make this the No. 1 destination." The rally ended with workers chanting, "Disney workers need a raise! Disney workers need a raise!"

At another rally not long afterward, hundreds of Disney workers, many in their work clothes, marched from a strip mall to an entertainment center at Disney World, passing a dozen hotels filled with tourists. They chanted, "Disney workers need a raise" and "1–2–3–4. Disney is a greedy whore" and carried red balloons that said, "End Disney Poverty." Some wore red T-shirts that said, "Disney workers need a raise."

"I think with cast members staying together, it will have a cumulative effect. There's no way it can't," said Jeremy Cruz-Haicken, who led Orlando's other large United Here local. "These negotiations have gone on for a long time. People are angry. People are living in poverty and they need some improvement in their lives."

Chambers still wasn't convinced the protests were having an impact on the Disney decision makers in getting what they wanted. "The people who make the decisions aren't looking at this," he said. "You know who this affects? The poor managers who have to come in here and referee this."

In spite of the protests and pressure the unions tried to put on Disney, negotiations continued with the company. Donna-Lynne was an old pro at the negotiating table. She had been doing contract negotiations on behalf of Disney workers for almost two decades. Disney officials and the union representatives sat at two long tables with the union representatives on one side and Disney officials on the other. Chairs surrounded the conference tables so rank-and-file Disney employees could watch the talks.

During negotiations with Disney officials lasting almost a year, each union had two or more representatives at the negotiating table. Clay, for the first time, had a seat at that table, having become head of the union local only a year earlier. Donna-Lynne noticed a problem with proposals that Clay had set on the conference table. Missing from the proposals were standard language at the bottom about the union's right to modify items during the negotiations, and Clay had miscategorized a job, placing it in the wrong union. Clay was supposed to send Donna-Lynne the proposals ahead of time to proofread them since she was the council's secretary-treasurer, but he had refused to do so out of spite. Donna-Lynne and her good friend Julee Jerkovich, an official with the food workers' union, ended up scribbling the missing language on dozens of copies of the contract proposals.[7]

Donna-Lynne Dalton stands in front of a Teamsters banner at the Local 385 hall in Orlando, Florida, in 2016. (AP Photo/ John Raoux)

Performers playing Mickey Mouse and Donald Duck wave from a float during a parade at the Magic Kingdom in Walt Disney World outside Orlando, Florida, in 2022. (AP Photo/ Ted Shaffrey)

Donna-Lynne Dalton sits at her desk at the Local 385 hall in Orlando, Florida, in 2016. (AP Photo/ John Raoux)

A performer dressed at Captain Hook from the "Peter Pan" story entertains a crowd at the Magic Kingdom in Walt Disney World outside Orlando, Florida, in 2022. (AP Photo/ Ted Shaffrey)

A character performer dressed as Goofy walks in a parade at Magic Kingdom in Walt Disney World outside Orlando, Florida, in 2022. (AP Photo/ Ted Shaffrey)

Ralph Singer, who drives trucks for the film industry, complains about the direction Local 385 is heading at a restaurant in Orlando's tourism hub in August 2017. (AP Photo/ John Raoux)

A protester dressed as a Power Ranger joins other unionized workers from Walt Disney World in protesting a contract proposal in the middle of Orlando's tourism district in 2022. (Photo by Phelan M. Ebenhack).

Former International Brotherhood of Teamsters president James P. Hoffa is seen in the East Room of the White House in Washington in 2015. (AP Photo/ Andrew Harnik)

Teamsters workers at Walt Disney World protest a contract proposal in the heart of Orlando's tourism hub in 2022. (Photo by Phelan M. Ebenhack)

Unionized Walt Disney World workers protest a contract proposal in a tourist hub outside Orlando, Florida, in 2022. (Photo by Phelan M. Ebenhack)

9

Unhappiness

The problems for Local 385, and increased worries about the health of union democracy at the local union, mounted once Clay Jeffries became president. No one was quite sure why Clay's predecessor, Mike Stapleton, had chosen Clay to succeed him. His appointment by Stapleton pleased some of the UPS drivers, but it was somewhat puzzling to members in other units in the local. However, the executive board of the local, including Donna-Lynne, under pressure, approved it unanimously, with Donna-Lynne actually "seconding" the motion.[1] Spike speculated that after a person worked for the Teamsters for a while, they cut corners or did things that were not always above board, and others who worked alongside them knew where the bodies were buried, so to speak. Spike believed that was why Stapleton picked Clay to succeed him.

"They're thick as thieves," said Teamsters member Steve Davison. Sitting with another Teamster truck driver, Ralph Singer, over lunch one day, Davison explained it like this. "Me and Ralphie work 20 years together, right or wrong, there are a lot of things that get done on the dock or on the road," said Davison, a freight truck driver. "Maybe I hit another trailer over the years. We all have dirt on each other over the years."[2]

In his first year as president of Local 385, Clay drew the scrutiny of federal labor judges by making it difficult for members to leave the union. An anti-union legal group had encouraged Local 385 members to leave the union over Clay's indifferent treatment of members. Lawyers for the National Right to Work Legal Defense Foundation started by showing Disney workers how to use a form letter to resign and demand that Local 385 stop deducting dues from their pay checks. Because Florida was a right-to-work state, Disney workers were under no obligation to be members of a union in order to benefit from the union contract. Workers, primarily character performers and bus drivers from Disney World, submitted their resignations to the Local 385 office and then waited and waited some more. They never heard back from Local 385, yet their dues kept getting deducted from their paychecks. The workers filed complaints against Local 385, with assistance from the anti-union foundation, alleging that the union was violating their rights by intentionally ignoring their requests to leave it. They said the union had breached their duty of fair representation and coerced their members to pay dues for a year or more after they had requested to leave. Clay responded that the workers had not followed the proper steps for requesting leave of the union local. At the time the workers filed their charges, Clay was secretary-treasurer of Local 385, which required him to process all membership dues and negotiate agreements; he would become president of the local shortly thereafter. Under onerous rules enforced by Clay, Disney workers had to make their requests to drop their union membership within a ten-to-twenty-day window before the anniversary of when they joined. If members wanted to leave the union, they had to put their request in writing only to Clay, who would acknowledge it with a written reply. Voicemail and phone message requests would not be recognized as sufficient notice for resigning. Other staffers in the union hall were prohibited from answering questions about membership forfeiture due to earlier problems in which staffers had given out misinformation.[3]

A Disney bus driver who wanted to leave the union called twenty times to see if Clay had gotten her resignation letter, but he never responded. Adding to the roadblocks, membership forms and authorization dues forms were kept as paper records, since efforts to store them electronically had caused the local's computers to crash. National Labor Relations Board investigators said that Clay repeatedly ignored the written requests and phone calls for information, claiming the requests had been misplaced or he never got them.

Local 385's attorney, Thomas Pilacek, said the workers weren't following the policy and Clay had no animus toward them. Pilacek said the complaints came from only a handful of the local's thousands of workers over two years. "It's perfectly reasonable that the case be in writing before it's responded to," Pilacek said.

At one of the worker rallies over contract negotiations with Disney World, an Associated Press reporter approached Clay. He hadn't returned any phone calls or email messages the reporter had sent him over the course of several months. Clay was a massive, obese guy, with red air and a thin mustache. He frowned when the reporter introduced himself and said he would love to hear his side of the story. "I'm not interested. I've been down this road with you," Clay said. That wasn't true, the reporter clarified. "We haven't talked. That's the problem. We haven't talked," said the reporter, but Clay cut him off. "The problem is you put a one-sided story out there," Clay said. The reporter offered to give him his business card and asked Clay to call him whenever he felt like telling his side. "I don't want it," Clay said.

According to University of Illinois labor scholar Steven Ashby, undemocratic unions leave themselves vulnerable to the tactics of anti-union organizations who target dissatisfied workers. And that is exactly what happened to Local 385. "The reality is that politics in America is corrupt," Ashby writes. "However, you don't fight corruption in politics by becoming equally corrupt. That corrupt reality should not subvert our ideals as unionists. The ends—doing good things for working people—do not justify undemocratic behavior."[4]

The National Right to Work Legal Defense Foundation's efforts targeting Clay and Local 385 were part of a larger anti-union movement that had developed over the past seventy years and aimed to damage the already crippled US labor movement in the last decades of the twentieth century and first decades of the twenty-first. By the 1950s and 1960s, many of the nation's largest unions were "internal oligarchies, administratively top-heavy with technicians and officials increasingly parochial in their bargaining strategy and political outlook," said Nelson Lichtenstein.[5] The decentralization of the US labor market, management hostility, and the relative weakness of the labor movement "generated a huge stratum of full-time officials, put a premium on authoritarian leadership, devalued independent politics and opened the door to a whole set of corruptions that became an integral part of the postwar mythos," he said. By the middle of last century, many unions had become entrenched bureaucracies, with union officials managing billions of dollars in pensions and health and welfare funds and doing so with some undemocratic impulses. They also became targets of Republican lawmakers and their conservative, usually southern, Democratic allies, who passed a series of laws in the late 1940s and 1950s curbing the power of unions. The Taft-Hartley Act was enacted in 1947 following a wave of strikes in postwar America. It prohibited "wildcat strikes"—unofficial protest work stoppages done without formal approval by union leadership—and secondary boycotts, when union workers refuse to do business with a company in a dispute with its workers, such as transportation workers refusing to transport goods made by a company whose workers are striking. Most significantly, the Taft-Hartley Act allowed states to pass "right-to-work" laws, which prohibited workers from being forced to pay union dues even if they were covered under a union contract. This was considered a direct attack on the strength of union membership.[6]

In 1959, lawmakers also passed the Landrum-Griffin Act in response to congressional hearings that had focused on corruption and mob-related influences in a handful of unions. The law strengthened parts of the Taft-Hartley Act and gave the US Department of Labor greater power to regulate the financial affairs of unions. It established a union member "Bill of Rights," which guaranteed that union members had the right to vote for leaders or referendums, attend meetings, and participate in union business.

Around the same time, anti-union right-to-work laws began springing up around the United States, and they particularly took a hold in southern states over the next half century. But the anti-union movement was static until the late aughts of the twenty-first century when a coalition of conservative and business interests started targeting formerly strong union states such as Indiana, Michigan, and Wisconsin for right-to-work laws. The right-to-work laws in general prohibited any requirement that employees enjoying the benefits of a union contract must be a member of the union.[7]

Around those efforts were formed a series of anti-union consultants and law firms whose business was based on showing companies how to keep unions out of their workforce or how to rid their labor forces of unions. One of the most prominent was the Labor Relations Institute (LRI), which said on its website, "Your Union Organizer Is Praying You Won't Find This Page."[8] Consultants for the firm, also called "persuaders," specialized in developing anti-union strategic campaigns for companies whose workers were on the verge of deciding to join one through an election. LRI said it was different from other consulting firms because, rather than focusing on bashing the union, it would try to help managers improve their performance so that workers would not want to join a union. The consultants advised companies to take advantage of the "captive audience" meetings workers were required to attend, which they deemed an advantage management had over union organizers, so they could hear management's views against unionization. They also recommended portraying unions as not looking after the interests of their members and affirming how it was better for managers to work together with employers without outside interference. Another union-busting firm, Sparta Solutions, advertised what it called "the art of positive employee relations, as well as union avoidance." The company said it was staffed with former union organizers, former union staffers, and former National Labor Relations Board staffers.

The union-busting consultant industry had been growing in the first two decades of the twenty-first century. The Economic Policy Institute estimated that companies each year spent $340 million on consultants who helped their companies stop unionizing. In many cases, the firms took an advance of only half their fee and promised companies they could keep the other half if the company lost a union election. Consultants were allowed to flood the workplace with anti-union communications. Supervisors were allowed to meet with workers and share anti-union messages, according to the Economic Policy Institute. Consultants were well-compensated for their efforts, with some union-busting consulting firms charging rates of $2,500 a day.[9]

Spike had interviewed with LRI but then decided to go with another firm. The way Spike described it, his job was to educate people about how not to get ripped off by unions. He said the anti-union consultant group that he joined in 2016 had treated him better than the Teamsters ever did. But the work could be dangerous at times. Once, on assignment for a health-care system in Springfield, Massachusetts, Spike was inside his hotel room, watching television and strumming his guitar, when he heard a rattling outside. He muted the television and sat there for a minute. When he did not hear anything else, he turned the TV back on. The next morning, in the hotel room's bathroom, he noticed white dust on the windowsill that resembled paint overspray. When he raised the blinds, he saw a bullet hole in the wall and a copper jacket on the floor. Police detectives who showed up at his hotel room characterized it as a stray bullet, but Spike viewed it as the union trying to send him a message. "Someone was sending me a message, 'We know where you're at,'" Spike said. "They obviously weren't trying to kill me. It's just all too weird."[10]

Anti-union consulting firms not only fought unions before they found homes in companies but also attacked unions once they were firmly entrenched in workplaces. One of the most visible of these firms was the National Right to Work Legal Defense Foundation, which, starting in the late 1960s, launched campaigns against what it called "compulsory unionism," primarily through litigation and education. In the 2010s, it set its sights on weakening unions at Disney theme parks, first at the Disneyland Resort in California, where it helped two workers at the Grand Californian Hotel & Spa file federal charges against a Unite Here local. The hotel workers claimed they were forced to pay full union dues even though they had refrained from joining a union. They were required to pay some dues for the union's efforts at collective bargaining, grievances, and contract enforcement but not the full amount if it involved activities such as political lobbying or members-only events. The National Right to Work Legal Defense Foundation then set its sights on Local 385 and what Clay was doing in Orlando.

In a ruling against Local 385, administrative law judge Michael Rosas described Clay as being "frequently vague and evasive" in his answers about why the Disney workers hadn't been able to leave the union. In the case of a Disney bus driver, the judge said Clay "was not credible" about whether he had known about the driver's request to leave the union and was "vague and hesitant." Clay's story about request letters being misplaced "was not credible either," the judge said. Regarding another character performer, the judge said Clay had no excuse for failing to respond to letters requesting an end to membership. Of another case involving a costumed performer, the judge said he found it hard to believe that Clay could not remember getting written requests and voice mails about her desire to leave the union, "which I find highly incredible and consistent with Jeffries pattern of ignoring resignation and revocation requests." The judge ordered Clay and Local 385 to cease and desist their efforts to ignore members' requests to leave the union and honor previous requests by members to end their union membership. The judge also ordered them to pay interest on the dues that the members were forced to pay against their will, and he forced them to mail notices to members that they would not fail to respond to requests to leave the union in the future.[11]

The notice read, "The National Labor Relations Board has found that we violated Federal labor law and has ordered us to post and obey this notice."

The individual Disney character performers and bus drivers who had been fighting to get out of the union were not the only members unhappy with Clay's leadership once he became president of Local 385 in 2016. Spike believed that once Clay became president of the local, he had it in for Donna-Lynne. Clay used to call Donna-Lynne "Casper," as in the ghost, since she hardly was in the union hall because of the animosity she felt directed at her and the large number of bargaining units she represented. "He just hated her," Spike said. "She's smarter than him. She's a woman."[12]

UPS driver Sean Mason was frustrated that Clay had not allowed steward elections. He believed that under Clay's leadership, "it had become just a dictatorship."[13]

Authority in the International Brotherhood of Teamsters was decentralized among its hundreds of local affiliates and joint councils, so the head of a local wielded tremendous power over the members in the local. Ralph

Singer, a movie driver and construction driver at Disney World, had been wanting to examine Local 385's financial books for years, but Clay and his associates refused to let him, even though he was a member in good standing and Teamsters bylaws allowed members to see them. When he brought up the matter at Local 385 meetings, Clay and other Local 385 members shushed him and told him to sit down.[14]

Labor scholar Steven Ashby has noted that the best way to keep union leaders from evolving into "prima donnas" is financial transparency. "The only answer is for complete financial transparency, a membership that monitors its leadership and a leadership that constantly monitors its own behavior and embraces members monitoring all union finances," he wrote.[15] In the summer of 2017, rumors began spreading among members that Clay had given a raise to himself and other Local 385 executive board members without the proper authorization and wasn't giving scholarship money raised for members' children to actual members. At monthly membership meetings, Ralph stood up, time after time, and asked Clay if he had given himself an unauthorized raise, and Clay would move on to the next order or business without acknowledging him. When other members asked Ralph what was going on, he told them, "They're stealing our money left and right and doing whatever they want."[16]

A driver like Ralph could earn $60,000 to $80,000 a year in what would be one of the higher-paying Teamsters jobs.[17] But working for the union local brought more money. When he first became president of Local 385 in 2016, Clay received a total compensation of $170,000 a year. Two years later, his annual compensation had reached $184,000. It was one of the few jobs in which a person without a college education could be making that kind of money. Plus, the local paid for leaders' vehicles and gave them credit cards.

Ralph viewed the Local 385 leaders as starting out as regular guys like him, then changing once they assumed leadership jobs in the union affiliate. "They are truck drivers, and they make between $60,000 and $85,000 a year driving trucks. Then, they get into the union hall, and they're making between $110,000 and $120,000, or more," Ralph said. "With a car. With credit cards. They go to Las Vegas for the shows. They get so wrapped up in the whole thing that they think after four or five years, nobody is going to notice. 'The building is paid for. We've got plenty of money.' And then, that's how it starts. They give themselves raises. They buy new cars."[18]

Ashby, the labor scholar, again, has warned of the dangers of leaders alienating members by taking excessive salaries as well as other perks. In the past, top leaders at other unions around the United States had used members' dues to install hot tubs in their offices, hold meetings at posh resorts in Florida and California, and drive around in stretch limousines. "Excessive salaries are not just antithetical to union values; they also aid employers' anti-union drives," he writes. "Whenever workers launch a union drive at their worksite, management or their union-busting consultants inevitably bring up the salaries of top union leaders paid by members' dues."[19]

Meanwhile, Local 385 was hemorrhaging members, including those from about half a dozen law enforcement agencies, who had voted to leave. "This is the worst I've ever seen a local run in my entire career, and I come from the northeast, New York and Connecticut, and that's a pretty tall standard," Ralph said. The way Ralph saw it, with more than nine thousand workers, Local 385 was a cash cow and the International Brotherhood of Teamsters in Washington, DC, did not want to change the status quo. At the time, Local 385 was annually collecting almost $3.6 million in dues and fees—an average of $400 per member—and had $2.3 million in net assets.

"A large percentage of members' dues, sometimes more than fifty percent, go to the state or district offices and to the international union," Ashby writes. "Regional bodies can be extremely helpful to local unions by providing experienced bargainers to assist in contract negotiations, training for new officers, organizers to assist forming new local unions and by offering educational classes for members on building stronger unions. But do unions' national headquarters need massive budgets? . . . Would much of that money be better spent by local unions and regional bodies hiring 44 more organizers and union representatives?"[20]

When Mike Stapleton was running Local 385, the members had a voice. With Clay, "there's no more of that," Ralph said. Every decision was being made behind closed doors, there was no transparency, and Ralph believed no one could challenge Clay. Ralph also could not get anyone from the International Brotherhood of Teamsters in Washington, DC, to return his calls when he left messages complaining about what was going on at Local 385. For months, he had been trying to talk to someone at headquarters who would listen to him about what he thought were misdeeds at Local 385. But they were getting tired of him. "Because they've got plenty of money, nobody cares," Ralph said.

Ralph first tried the Teamsters Union's internal top investigator. After he emailed the investigator in the summer of 2017, threatening to file a complaint with the independent review board, the investigator called him back within half an hour, telling him he shouldn't do that, according to Ralph. Soon after Ralph got off the phone, Clay called him. The internal investigators had told Clay about the call, and Clay told Ralph, "I know what you're doing. It ain't going to work." Ralph finally filed a complaint with investigators from the independent review board, accusing Clay of giving himself a $400 a week raise without executive committee approval. In early August 2017, Ralph sent documents to the IRB and an investigator interviewed him over the phone.[21]

"It's important to have the review board to keep the Teamsters honest," Ralph said. "We obviously cannot review ourselves and police ourselves and that has been proven time and time again. Is it costly for the union to have the IRB? Yes, but it's necessary for our union, for our viability."

Ralph was a big guy with a long face, a tall frame, big hands, and a wide smile. He first joined the Teamsters in 1983 as a truck driver in Connecticut and transferred to Florida in 2004. He got involved with Local 385, which also worked on movies and gas pipelines. Then, he started driving trailer trucks for the movies, which was his favorite job. Otherwise, he was working at Disney World's construction arm driving dump trucks and hauling heavy equipment.

Sean Mason saw Local 385 turning into a small dictatorship. He had been pushing for steward elections among his fellow UPS drivers, but Clay would not do anything about it. He was also upset by what he believed had happened with scholarship money that should have gone to the children of other members; that hadn't happened and no one knew where the money went. Sean had lost faith in Local 385 and thought it was turning authoritarian. "We don't trust our local, which is sad," Sean said.[22] Steve Davison, the YRC driver, said every year he posted at his work's bulletin board information about the Teamster scholarship fund. "I've never had one of our guys get it."[23]

An audit of Local 385's finances earlier in the year had found problems. The auditor marked "no" in the form where it asked if the local was following sound internal financial controls and complying with the Teamsters Union's financial practices and if receipts accurately reflected the local's records. The audit instructed the local to create a separate scholarship fund instead of putting money donated by members for scholarships in the general fund. "Must improve all internal controls surrounding handling of scholarship fund," the audit said.[24]

Donna-Lynne also had reached out to investigators over Clay's behavior, but her position was more precarious than Ralph's since she was a part of Local 385's executive board. Clay couldn't find out she had reached out to investigators or else she would be in serious trouble and possibly lose her job with Local 385.

The Local 385 leadership had asked the employers of Teamsters members and other unions to donate to the scholarship fund, and essays had been submitted for the scholarship. But she was worried the members' kids were not getting the scholarships. She reported her concerns to the Teamsters Union in March 2017, but the union did not do anything. "This is corruption," she said. Not only did the Teamsters Union not do anything, but officials there told Clay that Donna-Lynne had been complaining about him. She then filed complaints with the IRB and the Department of Labor. Like Ralph, Donna-Lynne hoped the local would be put into trusteeship and Clay would be removed.

After a few board meetings, Clay asked Donna-Lynne to change the minutes of the meetings. Clay told her that she needed to put in the minutes that the executive board had reviewed and amended the referral hall rules for people who are sent out to work at the convention centers and Disney warehouses. Donna-Lynne refused to do it because they did not amend anything. Clay said they had changed it to require nonmembers who used the referral hall to get jobs to work one hundred hours instead of ten hours to get a vote in local elections. The reason he wanted this change, Donna-Lynne believed, was the upcoming election year. The change would result in fewer members who were eligible to vote and would also allow the Local 385 to keep extra money paid by people who are not members but used the referral hall to get jobs. The Local 385 executive board also made two new hires during a meeting after Clay had been picked as president—Chris Gonzalez and Gary Brown, who was doing a second stint at the union affiliate.[25]

Donna-Lynne got confirmation about her suspicions on the pay raises not long after when she went to Laura Stapleton to get a file for verifying the number of hours she had worked. Laura accidentally gave her the file of one of Clay's lieutenants, and Donna-Lynne found out that Clay and other members of the executive board had gotten pay raises while she had not. "I had more responsibility, more seniority, more members. I negotiate my own contracts. I have more education. And I was now paid less," Donna-Lynne said.

Donna-Lynne emailed another Local 385 official to ask if the scholarships had been awarded and got a reply of "no." Donna-Lynne knew that was bad. The local had held a golf tournament to raise money for the scholarships and they had accepted donations for them. Where was that money going? Donna-Lynne reached out to the Teamsters internal top investigator. He promised to look into her concerns and urged Donna-Lynne to send him any supporting information.

"I need you to be patient," the investigator emailed back. "Keep your head down and mouth closed. The last thing I want is for you to get fired for some stupid reason. Go to work, do your job and listen and anything you hear that may be important please let me know."

Donna-Lynne confided to the investigator about the hostile and harassing working environment she was facing at Local 385's union hall. The investigator recommended that she hire an outside attorney, which rubbed Donna-Lynne the wrong way.

"I find it sad that I should have to go to someone on the outside and angry that I should have to bear the financial burden to get justice when I tirelessly fight these very same issues as my duty as a union officer and agent on behalf of our members," Donna-Lynne wrote him back. "On a personal note, I have struggled with my decision not to pursue justice for many years because it contradicts my principles and violates my rights. I would be flabbergasted if any my children or members were in such a situation and didn't stand up and fight. I have managed to justify it to myself because I was protecting the respect for and perception of the union."

Around the same time, the independent Teamsters investigators, motivated by the complaints from Ralph and Donna-Lynne, finally launched a probe into Local 385. The investigators got subpoenas for the minutes of meetings, a membership roster, auto-lease agreements, cash receipts and disbursements, payroll records, contracts, and monthly bank statements.[26]

Donna-Lynne's relations with the other Local 385 leaders had gotten so tense that she had been avoiding the union hall so she did not have to encounter them. But she needed to drop off receipts one Friday in late August 2017 and that required an in-person visit. Only days earlier, Donna-Lynne had met secretly at an Orlando hotel with the independent Teamster investigators from New York, Jerry Pugh and Dan Healey, who had flown to Florida to meet with her and go through Local 385 documents. Without realizing it, the two independent investigators were now there in the union hall when Donna-Lynne stopped by on one of her rare visits. They were poring over documents about pay report sheets and scholarship memos. Donna-Lynne tried not to panic. Talk about bad timing; she was the reason they were there.

Donna-Lynne tried to avoid them, but when she was going to a janitor's closet to get some toilet paper, they saw her through the open conference room door. They waved, called out a "hello," and asked her a question about something in the documents they were looking at. Donna-Lynne gathered some folders she needed from her office and walked by the conference room again, hoping to remain invisible, when one of the investigators shouted into the hallway another question for her. She quickly slipped into the conference room and shut the door. Donna-Lynne gave him a curt answer and then left as quickly as she could.

Laura Stapleton had come down the stairs leading to the upstairs offices and saw her walking out of the conference room. "What are you doing in there?" Laura asked her. Donna-Lynne paused for a second and then said, "Oh, I don't know. I went in to ask who they were. Who are they?"

Laura stared and said slowly, "Investigators."

"Hmm," Donna-Lynne said, eyes widening, pretending to act surprised. Donna-Lynne wanted to throw Laura, and whoever else Laura might tell, off her scent. Donna-Lynne knew it was risky, but she went upstairs anyway into the office of Rom Dulskis, one of Clay's lieutenants, and said, "You didn't tell anybody on the executive board that those people are in the conference room?"

"Oh, it's just, they're doing an audit," he said. She felt like rubbing what was an obvious lie back in his face. "Well, that's funny because they told me they're looking at some files," Donna-Lynne said. "Laura told me they're investigators and you're telling me they're auditors when we just had an audit done?" She paused for effect, in pretend indignation, and in a facetious tone, she said, "Happy Friday!"[27]

That Tuesday, the day after Labor Day weekend in 2017, Clay was agitated, and for good reason, as he joined negotiators from the other unions for yet another round of contract talks with Disney officials in the hotel ballroom. He likely knew that Donna-Lynne was responsible for the Teamsters investigators' visit to the union hall. Adding to Clay's agitation was an Associated Press story that had run around the world over the weekend, spelling out a growing unhappiness with his leadership among rank-and-file members who were fed up with how the union of Mickey Mouse and Goofy was being operated. They accused Clay of giving himself unauthorized raises, making it difficult for members to leave, not allowing members to see the union's records, and other problems. He also had likely learned that Donna-Lynne was planning to challenge him for the top job in the local affiliate. She really did not want to run, but she did not see any alternative to a needed leadership change.

Rom Dulskis was at the contract negotiations that day, and that struck Donna-Lynne as odd since he had nothing to do with representing the Disney workers at that time. Since Rom had been in the offices when the independent investigators surprised them with a visit days earlier, Donna-Lynne decided to taunt him about it during a break for lunch. "You think the members should know what's going on?" she said, referring to the fact the union local was now obviously under investigation. By then, Clay and another top lieutenant, Walt Howard, a big husky former truck driver, had joined them in a huddle in the hotel ballroom used for negotiations. Donna-Lynne recalled that Rom told her that if anybody asked about the investigation, "Your comment is no comment." Donna-Lynne turned to the Teamsters men and said, "You all are not pulling me into your bullshit," and then walked out of the conference room and went to lunch with her stewards.

When the day's negotiations with Disney officials had wrapped up, and the union representatives were packing away their papers, Clay approached Donna-Lynne and said he and the other top officials of Local 385 needed to meet with her the next day. She said she had a prior commitment and could do it by phone. But Clay said it needed to be in person, and that's when Donna-Lynne suspected she was going to be fired. She was sure Clay now knew that she was behind the investigators coming to the union hall, and he clearly was now aware that she planned to run against him for the top job in the local even though she had tried to keep that under wraps.

When she got home that night, she told her teenage son, Austin, that he needed to help her clean out her SUV that was rented by the Teamsters. When Austin asked why, she told him, "Clay is going to fire me. Just because." But it was more than "just because." Clay rightly saw Donna-Lynne as a threat.

The next day at the Local 385 office, Clay told her, "We no longer need your services." She was asked to turn over her laptop and the keys to the SUV. "I'm going to need some boxes," she told him. Walt Howard was there and said, "I'll get you some boxes." She responded, "I bet you will." While she cleared out her office filled with Disney World mementos, Austin texted Donna-Lynne, "Did Clay fire you?" She answered back, "Yep." "Are you going to be OK?" he asked. "Yep," she responded.

Getting fired produced in Donna-Lynne a combination of relief and fury after a year of frustration with the direction her union local was heading.

There was relief over not having to work with the Teamsters men anymore, whom she had grown to loath because of their sexism and homophobia. But she was angry too, since she knew she was good at her job. She cared about the union members. There was also some comfort in knowing that she would be going back to a job she loved, working with the character performers at Disney World and rejoining her old colleagues in the theme parks.

"Unions properly run, with educated staff, serve a very important purpose in the workforce," Donna-Lynne said. "But to destroy everyone's dignity, respect, integrity . . ." Her voice trailed off.

10

Election

When word spread among the character performers that Donna-Lynne had been fired, some started crying. Others talked about leaving the Teamsters and joining another Teamsters local or a different union. "Donna-Lynne was our department's mom," said Steve Pollino, the costumed character performer. "She took care of everybody, everywhere, anywhere."[1]

Jonathan Sidwell, a longtime steward for the costumed character performers, lamented her departure, saying she always had the performers' backs. Like many cast members, Sidwell had once faced being fired by Disney for some transgression, and Donna-Lynne had come to his rescue. "She saved my job when I got fired unfairly," he said. "She fought for them to hire me back. She was always there for us."[2]

John Dodson, a long-standing performer who rose to be a union steward, said Donna-Lynne knew how to strike the right balance between representing the interests of the performers and acknowledging what was allowed in the contract with the company. "Donna-Lynne was one hundred percent committed," Dodson said. "She came up from our world, so she got it."[3]

After being fired, Donna-Lynne returned to being a worker in the theme parks with the costumed character performers she had represented, serving as a character performer, float driver and character captain who made sure the performers were safe and had what they needed when they were mingling with guests. Returning to the theme parks meant she would be making about one-third of the salary she had been earning with Local 385, but it was not all bad. She was returning to a job that she had loved with people who were like family members to her. It was like coming home, to be surrounded by directors, producers, puppet masters, performers, and dancers—creative people she had known for more than a quarter of a century. These were her people, and she felt much more comfortable with them than she ever had with the current leaders at the Local 385 union hall. She would not be representing her colleagues anymore, but she could still give them advice and help. "I left a job I loved to do, a job I believed in, and so it was not so terrible to go back to another job I love," she said. "There is no other job in the world when you have these moments when you have absolutely made someone's day and you have that genuine smile and joy." That feeling was reinforced about two weeks after she had returned to the parks. She was walking to her car in the employee parking lot, her legs aching from being on her feet all day, when the nightly Magic Kingdom firework show started. She crawled into her car, put the sunroof down, and watched the explosion of colors in the sky. "I thought, 'Yeah. This is a pretty good place to work,'" Donna-Lynne said.[4]

Now in her mid-fifties, Donna-Lynne also was almost twenty years older than she had been when she last worked in the parks. On some days, she would have all-night rehearsals and then would have to be back in the park the next day. On those days, Donna-Lynne and her coworkers would find an empty hotel ballroom at the Disney World resort to get a few hours of sleep before they had to show up for work. Remembering her younger days, when she did this on a regular basis, she thought, "How in God's name did I survive that? Because this is killing me. To be young again."

Meanwhile, Dodson, the longtime character steward, said that by switching back into the theme parks, Donna-Lynne was essentially starting over again, since she had been on an eighteen-year union leave and didn't have any vacation or benefits accrued over that time. "She was screwed by the Teamsters and she was screwed by the company. All her years of service with the company were gone. She had to start from scratch to earn everything again, for a very different role. Even though she's the business agent who negotiated all these roles. She lost everything on top of everything," Dodson said. "She was always there for her members, never had any bad business dealings. But she whistle-blew all the shit that was going on with the local and what do you do with someone who whistle-blows? You fire them so they're not around to tell the story."

Though she was no longer in the leadership of Local 385, Donna-Lynne was not giving up her Teamsters' card. She urged other Local 385 members to keep fighting for justice and union democracy and to stay Teamsters members. Donna-Lynne reminded them that she had filed complaints and that independent Teamsters investigators were probing Clay, and she urged members to be cautiously optimistic.

Before she was fired, several costumed character performers had approached Donna-Lynne, asking her to run for president of Local 385. Donna-Lynne just wanted to be left alone to do her job, but they were persistent in wanting someone to challenge Clay. Donna-Lynne hesitated since she did not want the additional responsibilities. Local 385 had started to bleed all kinds of members, who complained that Clay and his associates never called them back when they had a problem.

"This place is falling apart. It's crumbling," she said. Just that summer, Donna-Lynne was with her friend, Julee, at a rally over the Disney contract. Clay spoke in front of the members, and "it was such an embarrassment," she thought, since he looked like a sloppy man going through the motions. Donna-Lynne believed he lacked passion, commitment, and substance. He did not know the contract and did not know what he was talking about. "I was like, 'I cannot be a part of this anymore. I cannot be a part of who they are and what they're doing to the local.' I had some decisions to make," Donna-Lynne said.

Donna-Lynne had known Ralph Singer for a long time, because he had worked at Disney and was friends with Spike. Along with Ralph, Donna-Lynne was hoping the IRB would intervene and place the local in trusteeship so that there would not be an election in October. "Get these people out of here," she said.

Later that summer, in August, Donna-Lynne realized that the IRB was not going to intervene right away, so Donna-Lynne, Ralph, Sean Mason, the UPS driver, and other members fed up with Clay's behavior concluded they were going to have to put a slate together to challenge the incumbent Local 385 officers. Ralph did the recruiting legwork since Donna-Lynne was still on the executive board of Local 385 at the time, before she was fired. She could not let it be known that she was challenging Clay—at least not right away.

This would be the first challenge to an incumbent group of Local 385 officers in almost two decades, and some people were worried about retribution. No one had challenged Stapleton; he was too powerful a president and also was beloved by UPS drivers.

"An additional undemocratic practice is when members are pressured not to run to be a convention delegate or for the union's executive board because the leadership has a slate and wants an uncontested election to show the union's 'unity,'" writes Ashby, the labor scholar. "If there were no contested elections in US political elections, the American people would rightly decry the end of democracy. The same sentiment applies to union elections."[5]

Ralph and Donna-Lynne first thought about contacting the Teamsters for a Democratic Union (TDU) for help. But Donna-Lynne had been a longtime Hoffa supporter and worried that involving the TDU would take the focus off the local and its members and turn it into a "Hoffa versus Teamsters for a Democratic Union" fight. "We have to worry about our local, and our local is comprised of all of these members—Black, white, gay, straight, TDU, Hoffa. It doesn't matter. That's who we have to represent," Donna-Lynne said. "Everyone needs to focus on our local and get it right again."

By Labor Day weekend in 2017, Ralph had put a slate together that pulled representatives from the various job sectors that Local 385 represented. There was Ceia Collins from the Disney bus drivers; Sean Mason and Steven Gill from the UPS drivers; Karelyn Martin from Disney warehouses; and Steve Davison from drivers from YRC Freight. Donna-Lynne represented the entertainment workers, as well as launderers, ranch hands, and others, at Disney; and Ralph Singer represented the drivers at Disney's construction arm. They called themselves the "Members First" slate.

They all met at Ralph's house over Labor Day weekend to plan the campaign, but Collins was acting strangely. She kept going outside to talk on her phone. Two weeks later, after the Members First slate had been nominated and made public, Collins quit the slate, saying she did not want to be a part of it. Members First was now left without a representative for the bus drivers, a very important segment of Local 385 voters. Donna-Lynne believed Collins had secretly plotted with Clay's Unity slate the whole time to leave their team so they would have a bus driver vacancy on the ticket. "It was definitely to diminish our slate," Donna-Lynne said.[6] Ralph took a more generous view and believed Collins had been intimidated by Local 385 leaders who threatened to take away her job as a steward for the bus drivers.[7]

Clay and his Unity slate were not done trying to make life difficult for their opposition. They successfully pushed to get Ralph disqualified from being on the Members First ballot, claiming he was ineligible because he had not properly paid his union dues for the previous two years. The reason for that was his employer had not sent in monthly money from his dues check. Instead of paying each month, the company sent it in one big check for the year. It should not have mattered anyway, because the Local 385 election rules said members should not lose "good standing" just because an employer had failed to make a proper deduction for membership dues. On this matter, inaction by the Teamsters Union played in Clay's favor. When Clay challenged Ralph's eligibility, Ralph appealed it to the general president's office of James Hoffa. But the Teamsters Union attorney failed to respond with an answer of "yeah or nay," and the ballots were sent out to Local 385 voters without Ralph's name on them. With Ralph now off the ballots in addition to Collins, the Members First slate was forced to run with only five candidates instead of the planned seven, entering the campaign at a disadvantage with two people down.

On top of that, numerous supporters of the Members First slate reported not receiving their ballots. Members who were supposed to call a hotline to request their ballots found that the voicemail box was full all the time, so they could not leave messages. The members who failed to get ballots were mostly costumed character performers, who were supportive of Donna-Lynne's candidacy and UPS drivers. "Some people don't immediately recognize a conspiracy. It's like, 'What's wrong with these phones?'" Donna-Lynne said.

Clay was supposed to allow Donna-Lynne and her slate to proofread the ballots before they were sent out, and he was also supposed to notify her when the ballots were being mailed. He did neither, according to the Members First slate. Members First also was supposed to get the addresses of all the members in Local 385 so they could be sent out printed advertisements, but the printer did not send out the Members First mailers. Clay and his slate used the same printer, and they sent out his slate's mailers on the same day the ballots were mailed out. Disney bus drivers also said they were intimidated by their business representative and worried about the repercussions of not voting for Clay's slate.

On the Members First Facebook campaign page, costumed character performers gave testimonials about how Donna-Lynne had saved their jobs and had their backs over the previous twenty years. One of them, Andrea Zangara, wrote, "In my opinion, the other Teamster Slate is the perfect representation of the bad views that critics often have of the Teamsters and unions. Corruption just being one of the views that often come to mind." Donna-Lynne created a video showing people how to vote and mail it in. "Your vote is your voice. Make the right choice," the video said.

About two weeks before the election, the Members First slate posted on its Facebook page, "Vote to clean out the corruption and nepotism of the incumbent slate, make your voice heard and vote for the slate that will represent you as you should be represented, will speak up and fight for you, our brothers and sisters and foundation of our union."

Besides aiming to eliminate Clay from the leadership of Local 385, the Members First slate also proposed reducing officers' salaries, from the

$150,000 range to the $70,000 to $80,000 range, so that more business representatives could be hired to represent the members. They also tried to put a realistic spin on the chances of getting Disney to agree to a minimum wage of fifteen dollars an hour. The Members First slate was not sure that could be done. "When I was campaigning, I told them the truth and they probably didn't like that," Ralph said. Ralph thought the Members First slate had the potential to really help members where it mattered most. He envisioned the union offering English lessons since about half of the membership was born outside the United States. He believed the local could offer truck-driving lessons and forklift-driving lessons to help members advance their careers. "This union could be great. We could do so much," Ralph said.

Taking a page out of David Letterman's old television show, the Members First slate also posted a top 10 reasons members should vote for them. The list included the damning facts that Clay had never been elected to office and charges had been filed in labor court against the local under his watch for failing to respond to members. Clay and his associates had given themselves raises, the Members First slate pointed out, hundreds of members had left the union on their watch, and Clay had refused to hold steward elections.

"It's time to take YOUR local back and start making it about the MEMBERS FIRST again!" their posting said. "You can fix all of these things, but you MUST vote. Help us to restore our local to the proud, powerful union it once was!"

After the votes were counted, the Members First slate ended up getting only 41 percent of the vote, though its supporters believed they came up short because of dirty tricks and intimidation. "Not everybody got a ballot," said Steve Pollino, a costumed character. "They did every dirty, underhanded thing that they could so that we couldn't get the word out," Ralph said.

As labor scholar George Strauss has observed, incumbents in leadership positions can campaign full-time as part of their jobs, while their opponents lack those advantages as well as the levers of internal communication among members.[8]

"People were afraid, intimidated; even though it's a secret ballot, people don't believe that," Donna-Lynne said. "It appears they targeted pockets of members where ballots weren't mailed. There was a clump of character performers, there was a group of UPS drivers who can't stand Rom and Clay, who didn't get ballots. So, when you look at where these complaints came from to us, you see, 'Well isn't it convenient that this group obviously is supporting us,' but there are all these stumbling blocks in that."

Some members were despondent that Clay had won the election. "I'm sorry you guys didn't prevail," Garfield Geddes posted to the Members First team. "I'm lost in limbo with Clay not returning my calls or updating me on my case. It's been six months since he had the decency to address my situation."

11

Retaliation

Clay swiftly went after anybody who had opposed his reelection. Clay had previously told Spike's friend, Roger Allain, "Anybody who runs against me will pay for it." Without any help from International headquarters and with foot-dragging from the independent investigators, the Local 385 members who had run against Clay felt hung out to dry.

Clay started off by taking Donna-Lynne off the Service Trades Council Union, which she had served on as secretary-treasurer for years and maintained her position on even after getting fired from the Teamsters. He removed Sean as a UPS steward. Then, he took a longtime experienced steward for the costumed character performers, Donnita Coleman-DuBell, off the negotiations for the new contract. Donnita had helped negotiate four previous contracts but had backed Donna-Lynne, so in Clay's eyes, she had to go. "He's going to destroy the local. He's going to destroy the council," Donna-Lynne thought. Not long afterward, Donna-Lynne's phone was hacked. Someone used a computer program to make sure she got a robocall several times a day. "They are petty and vindictive and childish," Donna-Lynne said. "They're just lashing out in whatever way they can. Neither Ralph nor Sean have done anything other than stand up for the members."[1]

Ken Fisher, a well-liked UPS steward, was removed from his post because he had campaigned for Donna-Lynne and her team, as was another UPS steward. "They're crucifying us," Ralph said. "Anybody who supported our slate will now pay. Now that Clay has won, he is crushing everyone. Anybody he doesn't get along with, they get fired."

The Teamsters Union, once again, would not accept Ralph's calls, and officials there seemed to be turning on him after he gave an interview to the Associated Press about problems at Local 385. One of the attorneys in Washington, DC, told Ralph, "You've embarrassed us."

Even the independent investigators wouldn't talk to Ralph anymore because he had spoken publicly about the problems. Trying to kick him out,

Local 385 leaders sent a registered letter to Ralph saying he was no longer a member. "They're investigating. I get it," Ralph said. "But we're not getting any input at all. The International has kind of blocked us out since we lost the election. They don't want to hear from us."[2]

The Local 385 members were told repeatedly by the independent investigators that charges were coming against the local's leaders, but nothing happened. "It's all payback for me turning them in and running against them," Ralph said. "Clay thinks he is untouchable. Anybody who ran against him, anybody who reported on him, he's trying to crucify. So far, he's succeeding."

Clay and his colleagues were freezing out anybody who had supported Donna-Lynne and her team. With the YRC Freight, Teamsters' dues deductions were accidentally made twice, and members were unhappy with the extra money taken out of their accounts. When Steve Davison tried to fix the issue, the officers at Local 385 kept bouncing him around to different people, undermining his authority as a steward. "It's a little game they got back and forth, which makes you look weak to your members because you can't get them answers," Davison said.[3]

Roger Allain, Spike's good friend, had represented freight and convention workers for Local 385, but he was out on workers' compensation following a car accident. Eventually, Clay told him not to come to work since he was under doctor's order not to lift twenty pounds, even though working as a business agent wouldn't involve any heavy lifting. Roger went to the union hall to get a box of his belongings, and he got into a confrontation with one of Clay's allies, Gary Brown. Brown filed a criminal complaint against Roger, and Roger was charged with misdemeanor assault. The leaders of the Members First slate believed the whole thing had been a setup, meant to create an excuse to kick Roger out of the Teamsters and get him banned from being able to work on movie productions. Prosecutors dropped the charge the following year, and Roger was sent to a pretrial diversion program.[4] Donna-Lynne and other Members First leaders feared the same thing might happen to them, that somehow the Local 385 leaders would create a situation where trumped-up charges could be filed against them too as punishment for running on the Members First slate.

Then, there was the lack of effort exerted by the Local 385 leaders on basic contracts. They hadn't even signed a contract on a movie Ralph and other drivers were already working on. As a result, a Teamsters business agent from a South Florida local ended up filling the vacuum created by Clay's inertia.[5] He brought up his Teamsters members from Miami to work on the production. Fed up with members from another local taking the Orlando jobs, several of the Teamsters drivers for movies in Orlando moved to Atlanta, where there was more film and television production. Teamsters' members were complaining on the Members First Facebook page.

One Teamster member, Tracy Burridge, said that the Local 385 leaders were avoiding his calls over membership dues. "As is my concern, I do believe the people in the hall right now are committing fraud against their members," he said. "Donna-Lynne is the only person in the union who ever showed me any form of dignity. Everyone else I've spoken to, excluding the shop stewards, treated me like a revenue source that they didn't want to lose."

During a Local 385 membership meeting in April 2018, some members complained to Clay and his colleagues that the union was failing to abide by its bylaws by refusing to hold steward elections. "The ability to choose your representatives is a fundamental right of Union members, yet it is rarely acknowledged by the current Executive Board. This may explain the number of people who have decertified Teamsters Local #385 as their bargaining agent," some members wrote on the Local 385 Facebook page.

When those members were asked to "meet upstairs" to talk about the issue with Clay and other Local 385 leaders, they were told that the local wasn't inclined to help them because they were "seen talking to 2 fucksticks," referring to leaders of the Members First slate, including Donna-Lynne. "Most disturbingly it came to light that the current Executive Board of OUR Local is under investigation by the Independent Investigation Office," the members wrote, referring to the new name for the IRB. "The IIO is authorized by the consent decree to root out corruption. We aren't sure where this investigation will lead, but it's not a proud moment for our local to even be on the radar of an office tasked with ridding the Union of corruption. Please don't hesitate to talk to your fellow members and stay informed about what's going on in YOUR Union! Together we will ensure that eventually Teamsters Local #385 will put the MEMBERS FIRST!"

When attending meetings now, the members who had run on the Members First slate felt like daggers were aimed at them. "It used to be a brotherhood," Steve Davison said. "Now when I go there, the tension and hostility is something else."[6] Ralph's wife started worrying for his safety.

"I'm one of the most hated men in the local and the International," Ralph said. "But I'm OK with it. My wife, she watches too many movies. She says, 'They're going to come after you. They're going to kill you.' I say, 'No, that's not the way it works.'"

Character performers took Donna-Lynne aside and told her they wanted out of the Teamsters. After she had left, the costumed character performers felt that the leadership at Local 385 had cut off communications with them. "We saw Clay at the first meeting with stewards and it was like talking to a tree, basically," said Jonathan Sidwell, a longtime steward for the characters. "He just sat there smug as a bug and hardly said anything." When Sidwell would call Local 385 wanting to file a grievance on behalf of a member, he would not hear back from anyone.[7] "Grievances went unanswered. People were suspended and hung out to dry," said Teresa Freeman, the veteran costumed character. "People were waiting and waiting and waiting, and nothing."

When Sidwell ran into Rom Dulskis in a backstage hallway at Disney World and asked why no one was getting back to him, he was told point-blank that it was because he had supported Donna-Lynne. "I asked, 'Why are you treating us like that,'" Sidwell said. "And Rom said, 'Because you are one of Donna-Lynne's lackies. You were part of Donna-Lynne's crew.' And they were going to push us aside. I was told we were the redheaded stepchild now."

Some costumed character performers were hunting for another union that would take them. For Freeman, the last straw was when she heard one of Local 385's leaders say, "Entertainment can go screw themselves." Entertainment was shorthand for the costumed character performers. "Yeah, I don't need these people representing me because they don't care," Freeman said. "With that lack of care, that means management doesn't care either."[8]

Donna-Lynne warned them that trying to switch to a different union was a bad idea, and she found herself in the awkward position of encouraging members to stick with Local 385. "Characters don't want out of the union. They want out of Teamsters," Donna-Lynne said. "I'm like, 'No, you do not want out of the union. Do not forfeit your union membership.'"

Donna-Lynne also knew that it would be virtually impossible for the character performers to join another union in the Service Trades Council Union, since whichever union took them would appear to be poaching Teamsters' members. She couldn't be seen as fomenting that type of rebellion. "Realistically, if you do that sort of thing against another union's local, you are absolutely starting a civil war," she said. But the costumed character performers thought they had some leverage, given their importance in the Disney theme parks' ecology.

"The entertainment department is the biggest draw for anybody who walks into the parks, from the parades to the shows," Sidwell said. "They don't come here for the Mexico Pavilion or the France Pavilion. The come here because of Mickey Mouse, Pluto and the parades. All the big shows."

Still, Donna-Lynne urged them not to give up. "Now is not the time to give up on OUR local. WE must remember that WE are the union. WE must continue to stand up for what is right," Donna-Lynne wrote on the Members First Facebook page. "Karma may not be swift . . . but it is just."[9]

About a month after the Local 385 elections, the Disney workers who were Service Trades Council Union members took a first vote and rejected a contract proposal from Disney that would have raised wages by either 3 percent or fifty cents an hour, whichever was higher, twice over the life of the two-year contract. Disney also proposed giving all workers a $200 bonus. More than 90 percent of the dues-paying members rejected the offer. "We deserve more than 50 cents," Krystle Karnofsky, who earned ten dollars an hour working in Animal Kingdom, told the *Orlando Sentinel*. "We're not going to settle."[10] Donna-Lynne had her suspicions that the election was not completely above board. She felt that Clay and the two leaders of the Unite Here unions wanted the proposal rejected so they could come back to their members and say they were fighting for higher wages, as all of them faced upcoming reelection battles. Ballot boxes were set up in cast member cafeterias and break rooms at the Magic Kingdom and ballrooms at various resorts on the Disney World property. Often, the ballot boxes were cardboard boxes that were unsealed, and some costumed character performers felt intimidated to vote "no" when they cast their ballots. Some members of the Service Trades Council Union were treating Donna-Lynne as a pariah. Some bus drivers, working at a poll, gave costumed character performers a wood nickel when they voted, saying, "Here's your raise from Donna-Lynne."

12

Mickey Mouse Revolts

Within two months of the Local 385 election, hundreds of costumed character performers were demanding in a petition that Donna-Lynne be brought back as their union representative, and they threatened jumping to another union. The petition was signed by almost two-thirds of the one thousand costumed character performers and others who worked in the character department. "We the Walt Disney World characters, attendants and ranch hands stand united in agreeing a change needs to be made in our representation on the Service Trades Council," the petition began. "This is based on the lack of support and interest from our president, Clay Jeffries. The activities currently being investigated regarding the actions of the president, vice president and treasurer of our Local 385 have made us lose trust in the union and the people running it. The wrongful termination of our business agent, Donna-Lynne Dalton, has taken the only member of the local away that has fought for our rights and had influence in our negotiations."[1]

The threat from the costumed character performers got the attention of James Hoffa in Washington, DC, and he sent two representatives to Orlando to straighten things out with the characters. These Hoffa representatives were different from the investigators sent from the Teamster's independent investigative arm out of New York. The New York investigators were under the supervision of the federal court and were looking for criminal misconduct. Hoffa's personal representatives from the Teamsters Union, Mike Clarke and Dennis Morgan, were sent to Orlando to smooth things over. They immediately called for a meeting between the stewards for the character performers and the Local 385 leadership in early 2018. But the stewards for the character performers were wary about talking to Clay or his associate, Walt Howard, who had taken over representing the characters after Donna-Lynne was fired. During the meeting at a hotel near Disney World, the stewards felt like the Local 385 leaders had no interest in the character performers and were only trying to save face in front of Hoffa's people.

"Their concern is the characters are high profile to General President Hoffa, and this doesn't look good," Donna-Lynne said. "These people are not here to help and find an actual resolution. They are only here to save Mickey Mouse as a Teamster. And everyone finds that extremely offensive."

Morgan and Clarke were there to talk to the character performers. Persuading them to stay with Local 385 would be another matter. "The characters are a different breed," Donna-Lynne said. "The Teamsters don't realize these aren't assembly-line workers or truck drivers. Something like 92 percent of the characters have a college education. These are not uneducated people. They are there because they want to be performers. They want to be in entertainment." To suggest what Hoffa should be thinking about, Donna-Lynne said, "You better send someone down there and take it over before it becomes worldwide news that Mickey Mouse wants out of the Teamsters."[2]

Many of the members got the sense that the representatives from the Teamsters Union were there only to keep the peace with the characters and not really to address the undemocratic actions and substantive problems members were facing with the local leaders. They seemed more like mediators than investigators. "We're giving them this opportunity to correct this issue, but we're not seeing the other side bend," said Joe Maseda, a onetime chief steward in the Animal Kingdom character department who had become a manager.

Howard did not come from an entertainment background, and that lack of experience was showing now that he was representing the character performers. "Take surface areas, dance surface areas. If certain products are used, they can damage cast members' shoes, and you can injure yourself," Maseda said. "Or say you're dancing onstage and they give you the wrong shoes. You can injure yourself. Not knowing there's a specific shoe you need, you're not going to be able to fight for us."

Maseda said it was the same with other workers like float drivers. There were problems if the union business agent did not know what the workers' needs were. "Basically, when they decided to terminate Donna-Lynne, they never took interest in our department. She was the only one who fought for us," Maseda said. "They were basically using her as a scapegoat. The reason we do what we do now is because of her. We learned from her."[3]

The Hoffa representatives started a meeting with the stewards by asking everyone to go around the room and say how long they had worked at Disney World and been a Teamster. Maseda stopped them, saying that it was not necessary and they should just cut to the chase. Maseda had brought a copy of the subpoena from the investigators and documents and emails from unhappy members to read to the Hoffa representatives about how the local leaders were not returning their phone calls or doing anything to represent them. The Local 385 leaders at the meeting, particularly Howard, were defensive and accused the stewards of being selfish and disloyal. They also made disparaging, untrue remarks about Donna-Lynne, blaming her for the dissatisfaction among the character performers.

Donnita Coleman-DuBell, a veteran steward for the character performers, was at the meeting even though she had just been removed from the contract negotiating team because of her support for Donna-Lynne's team. She had been at Disney World for twenty-seven years, a Teamster for twenty years, and a contract negotiator for the costumed character performers for almost two decades. She was still fuming about the Local 385 leaders kicking her off the negotiating committee. "It got to the point where I felt like I wasn't being heard," Donnita said. "Everything with my local was disheartening. I had had enough of the bull."

Donnita said the Local 385 leaders had been doing everything wrong since they fired Donna-Lynne, and they were offending gay character actors by calling them disparaging names. "When it comes time to represent their members, they don't know how," Donnita said. "They get rid of our business agent of 18 years, who did an amazing job, and then they don't tap into their stewards and instead alienate them. Why wouldn't you reach out to me when you need your costumed characters? To make disparaging comments about anyone who is LGBT, and of course the majority of the cast members are of that community?"

At the steward meeting organized by Hoffa's representatives, Donnita had had enough and decided she did not want anything more to do with Local 385. In the heat of the moment, she stood up in the middle of the meeting and said, "I forfeit my membership. I've got to go." She did not really mean it, but she was just so upset. Howard said, "I accept your resignation." Donnita gathered her belongings and stormed out of the union hall.

"At this point, I'm feeling, if I can't transfer to another local, or I can't affiliate with someone else, then I'm not going to be a Teamster," Donnita said. "It hurts me to say it, but I can't be a part of a local that is so corrupt and not honest with their members and just not doing what they should be doing. I thought it was amazing that the International reps were here, but you shouldn't be coming down here if your performers say they don't want to be Teamsters and you tell them they need to get along with their leaders. That is not your job. THEY are the problem."

She was frustrated. "I think it's sad that our Local 385 is so corrupt that people want to go somewhere else," she said. "A lot of people were upset when we lost Donna-Lynne. She did her job very well. She got a lot of jobs back."

Not long after that, Donnita got her paycheck and noticed that her Teamster dues had not been deducted. A notation on the check stub said she had opted out of union membership, even though she had never submitted a formal notice to leave the union. A few days later, she got a message from a Local 385 member with a screenshot of an email sent by Rom Dulskis of Local 385 to Disney World's payroll department stating Donnita was no longer eligible for membership and to stop deducting her dues. "I've been a Teamster for 20 years. I didn't opt out," Donnita said. "They decided to contact Disney on my behalf to say I'm no longer eligible because I said I was going to forfeit my membership. That is the game they are playing." To keep her membership eligible, Donnita sent in her dues by certified mail to Local 385's offices, since they weren't being deducted from her paycheck. "Now, it looks like they don't want me anymore," she said. "It is so sad. This is my union doing this to me when the union is supposed to be for the worker. It's blowing my mind that I'm going through this with my union."[4]

Some of the costumed character performers were putting out feelers to join another union in the Service Trades Council Union, but Ed Chambers, who headed the council, was not in favor of it. "Every time someone gets upset with a union rep and says, 'Hey, give me another union.' What am I going to do?" Chambers said. "I have 38,000 people here. Am I going to be swapping unions all day?"

Not long after the arrival of Hoffa's representatives, Local 385 held its monthly membership meeting at the union hall, and Hoffa's representatives from the Teamsters Union also sat in. The UPS drivers complained about not being allowed to hold steward elections, while others complained about how the person in charge of the hiring hall was playing favorites and the Local 385 leaders had gotten rid of stewards they didn't think were loyal to Clay. Members claimed they had been double charged for membership dues in the previous month and the local had done nothing to refund them. Clay blamed the problems on Donna-Lynne, who was sitting in the audience, this time as a regular local member.

"It was so sad. Sitting there, I was like 'Wow,'" Donna-Lynne said. "He has destroyed everything that people worked very hard to build—trust, respect and dignity—and this is just awful. But it felt great that the Teamsters

Union reps were here and seeing this. And they can see for themselves, this isn't Ralph who didn't get his way and is whining, or Spike, the bitter ex-employee stirring things up, or Donna-Lynne, the sore loser who didn't win the election."

Ralph was also at the meeting, which attracted about sixty members, double the usual attendance. He thought that the Teamsters Union representatives were there to make it seem like Hoffa and the union officials in Washington, DC, cared about what was going, when really they did not. Ralph also thought they seemed to care only about smoothing the feathers of the costumed character performers and not worrying about other members of Local 385. "If it doesn't get straightened out by the International, a lot of units are going to leave," Ralph said. "I think this is false hope. I think they are here for a dog and pony show. If they trusteed the local, the International doesn't get their cut. If it's trusteed, the International doesn't get their 20 percent of dues money. They don't want to lose that. It's all about the money. It used to be about the men. Now, it's about the money."[5]

At one point, Donna-Lynne ran into a Disney manager who used to sit across the table from her in grievance disputes, representing the company. They had been adversaries then, but the manager told Donna-Lynne, "I never thought I would say this, but I miss you. I had a grievance hearing today and those guys didn't know what they were doing. If you had been there, it would have been fixed."

A few days later, in March 2018, Donna-Lynne again met with Jerry Pugh and Dan Healey, the independent investigators from the Teamsters' investigative arm in New York. They kept telling her that charges would be filed against the leaders of Local 385, but so far, nothing had happened. Donna-Lynne gave sworn statements, under oath, to the investigators about what was happening at Local 385. She was worried enough about the consequences of her testimony that she did not want to stay at her house for the few days surrounding her deposition. "If some of these people lose their jobs, pensions, homes, they will want to strangle me," she said.

Donna-Lynne was having a hard time moving beyond what had happened to her with the Teamsters. Given her drop in salary, she knew she should consider other employment alternatives but felt paralyzed about doing anything until the investigations were resolved. She even had an offer to join Disney's labor relations team but had turned it down. "Until this investigation is complete, I feel that I can't move on," she said.

13

Contract

While the internal war within Local 385 was going on, Disney was flirting with accepting an agreement with the Service Trades Council Union for an eventual minimum wage of fifteen dollars an hour over four years, provided the unions agreed to concessions on vacations, overtime, and access to new employees during orientation. Upon hearing the offer in spring 2018, Chambers said it was dead on arrival. "It was an interesting concept but at the end of the day, we weren't interested in it," Chambers said. He sent out a text to his members that the cost of agreeing to the offer was too high when it came to concessions on overtime, transferring jobs, working holidays, and the rights of stewards.

Not long after that, Chambers stepped down as the head of the Service Trades Council Union. He needed surgery, would be on painkillers for a while, and was close to retirement anyway. So, it proved to be a good time to step away on his own terms.[1]

By August 2018, Disney negotiators and the Service Trades Council Union had reached a deal. The starting minimum wage would rise by almost half over the next three years to fifteen dollars an hour. In exchange, Disney won concessions, including on being able to use more part-time workers; under the current contract, slightly more than one-third of the union workforce could be part-timers, but that would be increased to almost two-fifths of the workforce in the new deal. New hires also would have to wait longer to switch jobs under the proposed deal. The previous contract allowed for a transfer after six months, but that would change to a year under the new contract. The workers also would be getting the long-promised $1,000 bonuses. Only a month earlier, Disney had agreed to raise the minimum wage of workers at its California park to fifteen dollars an hour.[2]

During the vote count, scores of union workers chanted "Union! Union!" and "Nah, nah, nah, nah, nah, nah, hey, hey, we got a raise!" as they waited for the votes to be counted at a hotel in the heart of Orlando's tourism district. "We got a fair deal," the Service Trades Council Union's new leader, Matt Hollis, told the workers after the vote was counted and a contract was finally approved. Hollis had taken over as leader of the coalition of unions after Chambers stepped down. Union officials said the new contract would have an impact outside of Walt Disney World as other nonunionized businesses in central Florida's low-wage service economy compete for tourism workers in a tight job market.

While the members of the Service Trades Council Union were happy, members of Local 385 who had stood up to Clay were getting anxious that the independent investigators had not taken any action yet. "They are not doing a good job of representing anybody, but especially entertainment, and we represent the brand of the company," said Phillip Newell, a veteran Disney worker in the character department.[3]

Sean Mason talked to Healey and asked why the investigators hadn't yet filed any charges. "We all have targets on our backs if you don't do something," Sean told the investigator. "Anybody who stands up to these locals is going to be put down."

Ralph had also expressed his concerns, in a heated exchange, to the other representative from the independent investigations office, Jerry Pugh. "I told him I had no faith in him," Ralph said, recounting the conversation. "'We came forward, gave you all the information, and a year and a half later, you've done nothing. They're still stealing money and you all don't give a shit.'"

14

Leaving

The close of 2018 also was a turning point for Donna-Lynne. In December, she was given an offer she could not refuse: she was asked to become a representative for the actors at Disney World who were members of the Actors' Equity Association. She gave her two weeks' notice to Disney after the new year.

"It hurts my heart that I'm leaving the character department," Donna-Lynne said. "But I just can't stay." Referring to Local 385 leaders, she said, "The organization is from hell. They are a good old boy network. They are more concerned about protecting their fringe benefits than representing the members, all the way to the top. There's nothing that a girl was going to change."[1]

Donna-Lynne was not going to see the end of her efforts to reform and restore union democracy at Local 385—at least not as a Teamster. That effort would fall to several character stewards who picked up the mantle of the fight she had started with Ralph Singer and Sean Mason. Donna-Lynne also was leaving Disney World. While working at the Teamsters, she had officially been on extended leave from Disney, even if that leave had lasted almost two decades. Moving to Actor's Equity would mean a clean break from Disney.

Even though she was leaving, Donna-Lynne felt that a piece of her would always be with the character department. Everyone who had ever been a character at Disney World was still a member of a large extended family. Even after a character actor had left the department, they were still invited to meetups at the Atlantic Dance Hall nightclub on the Disney World property or to ride roller coasters together.

Now it would be up to other members of the character department to finish the fight for union democracy that Donna-Lynne and the other reformers had started.

15

A Reckoning

Clay's ultimate misstep would be with the character scheduling captains. Without telling any of the costumed character performers, Clay secretly negotiated a side agreement to the new contract with Disney to exclude dozens of scheduling captains from coverage by Teamsters representation. He eliminated them from the Service Trades Council Union contract.[1] "The company and the IBT Local 385 agree that the job duties and functions encompassed within the scheduling work for the company's character department do not fit the jurisdictional contours of the IBT Local 385 bargaining unit and are beyond the jurisdiction of the STCU," said the memorandum of understanding dated September 2018.[2]

The scheduling captains were outraged. The scheduler positions were coveted jobs for experienced performers, since they gave them longevity in the character department. They were basically office jobs that allowed character performers to ease into another spot in the character department once their bodies were no longer agile enough to be performers or they wanted to give their bodies a break, or their looks no longer fit their roles. Being a character could get more strenuous the older a performer got, with the wear and tear that came with dancing or leading a parade in a costume. Becoming a scheduler allowed character performers to remain in the department as they got older and slower on their feet.

Because of the side agreement, they now would have to choose between staying in their jobs or remaining a Teamster. Many of them saw it as payback for supporting Donna-Lynne and her slate. "So, the character captains got screwed out of their jobs," Sean Mason said. "Clay sold out dozens of jobs. Clay wanted to screw over the characters by knocking the schedulers who were stewards and had supported Donna-Lynne out of the union."[3]

John Dodson was among those who got caught in the squeeze caused by the secret side agreement. He had to choose between keeping his job as a scheduling captain and staying a Teamster. He chose the Teamsters. "I feel like I was sold out by my local union leadership because they literally gave away my union job away. What union gives away jobs?" Dodson said. "We've always been proud Teamsters. I've always been a proud Teamster."

Although he was staying with the union, what had happened was giving him doubts. "Without these things happening, I would never have wanted to leave the Teamsters," Dodson said.

Now Dodson and other members of the character department were looking for a way out. They may have been slow to realize just how bad things had gotten, or they were hoping to ride out the situation. Dodson had helped out Donna-Lynne with business agent work, and he had a business agent badge that allowed him to go backstage and talk to performers whenever he wanted. After Donna-Lynne was fired, the Local 385 leaders revoked his badge. "Even though she's been gone a year, year and a half, this is still payback," Dodson said.[4]

By this point, many of the character performers had reached out to Donna-Lynne to see if they could join the Actors' Equity Association. They would call her and say, "Mom. Help!" But for Donna-Lynne, that was a nonstarter since there were prohibitions against unions raiding each other's members. She knew there could be big trouble if she made even the appearance of trying to recruit the costumed character performers to her new union.

"I cannot act on that in any way, shape or form," Donna-Lynne said. "Actors' Equity is part of the AFL-CIO. There are anti-raiding agreements. There is also my integrity and credibility. As much as I love many of the people in that department, I can't taint those waters." But her heart broke a little bit each time a character performer called her seeking help. "It's difficult for me. These are people I have known for 28 years. And this is a horrible battle they are facing," she said. "The character department is so fed up and exasperated, they are just reaching out to anything and everything that might help them."[5]

After Donna-Lynne's departure, a group of character department members led by Phillip Newell and Donnita Coleman-DuBell, who had stormed out of the meeting in exasperation, picked up the baton and continued the fight against the Local 385 leadership. Phillip Newell had been working in the character department for more than fifteen years. Bespectacled and skinny, Phillip spoke thoughtfully with a trace of a Tennessee accent he had from growing up in Chattanooga. He had not previously gotten involved with union politics, but he had a strong moral code, and the undemocratic measures at Local 385 had rubbed him the wrong way.

"We are proud to be Teamsters. Just like we love working at Disney, we love being represented by the Teamsters," Phillip Newell said. "You don't have to be a really smart person to know that things aren't adding up. They're not doing a good job representing anybody, but especially entertainment, and we represent the brand of the company. Mickey Mouse is upset, and you can't have that."

They filed a complaint with the National Labor Relations Board (NLRB). The complaint was later dismissed and then denied on appeal. The NLRB general counsel's office said there appeared to be no collusion between Local 385 and Disney World with their deal to eliminate the schedulers from the union contract. General Counsel Peter Barr Robb, a Trump appointee, wrote that there was no evidence the jobs were moved out of the union because of "anti-union animus or in retaliation of any alleged protected concerted activities of those bargaining unit employees adversely affected by the reassignment." Disney World had notified Local 385, or at least Clay, of its intent to remove the schedulers from union protection so there was no violation of labor law that mandated that companies bargain in good faith with workers' unions, the NLRB general counsel said.[6]

Once again, it seemed to the union members like another undemocratic move by Clay that was going unpunished. "The employer met and negotiated with the union resulting in the parties executing a memorandum of understanding addressing the impact of the employer's decision on the affected represented employees," Robb wrote.

In retrospect, the NLRB complaint was more a strategic mistake than anything. The costumed character performers had filed the complaint against Disney World when the real culprit was their union's leader. Dodson said the members never were informed about anything regarding these negotiations. "We were told by our local that our jobs were safe," he said.

As it turned out, the side agreement giving away the scheduler jobs was the final straw, and it got Hoffa's attention, again. Phillip Newell and Donnita sent another petition to Hoffa's office bearing the names of more than six hundred workers from the entertainment department threatening to forfeit their union membership. It was part of a series of emails they had sent, claiming they were receiving "horrible representation."

"All members who have signed this petition agree that if union dues are not put to use by protecting our job classifications, then we see no reason to continue supporting Teamsters," read an email from the character performers accompanying the petition. In another email to Hoffa, they wrote that no one in their department had been notified about the change in schedulers being removed from union representation.

"We pay union dues for our jobs to be protected within their union classifications and this change is a disservice to ALL union members as well as a misrepresentation of what we were voting for in recent contract talks," they said. "Our Entertainment Scheduling Department represents dozens of cast members who now have to face the decision of possibly accepting a nonunion job or lose an hourly premium by staying in their current 'status' and accepting less desirable positions in other theme park locations. These cast members have spent tens of thousands of dollars in dues during their decades of service believing that the union will protect their job classifications."

Even Hoffa's personal representatives were not getting any answers from the Local 385 leadership. So, in late February 2019, Hoffa appointed a three-member panel and scheduled a hearing for the following month over whether the Teamsters Union should take over Local 385 in a trusteeship. "I have received creditable allegations that actions by the current officers of Local 385 have jeopardized the local union by failing to enforce collective bargaining agreements and otherwise failing to act exclusively in the interests of membership," Hoffa said in a notice posted on the union hall's doors.

Chief among the reasons for the hearings, Hoffa said, was the agreement with Disney that Clay had negotiated excluding the scheduling captains from being covered by the Teamsters, without any vote by members. Hoffa also said he had received complaints that local leaders were not responsive to grievances by workers in the movie industry. Local 385 leaders had failed to designate stewards to monitor the contract enforcement for the movie workers, and in some cases, they had not even negotiated contracts covering movie productions, he said.

"A fundamental obligation of all union officials is the protection of the interests of the members of the union and preservation of the union's jurisdiction and bargaining rights," Hoffa wrote in the notice. "Moreover, a union is legally obligated to perform responsibly as the bargaining representative and enforce its terms in the manner that best protects the works covered thereunder."[7]

The trusteeship hearing was held on the last Saturday in March 2019, with almost three hundred Local 385 members showing up for the marathon, all-day session. Dozens of character performers, not in costume, showed up with the petition to leave the Teamsters, and bus drivers came to back up Clay and other Local 385 leaders. The Local 385 leaders were up to their usual tricks. When Phillip Newell and others from the character department arrived at the union hall, they were told by a Local 385 officer manning the front door that they were not on the members' list and could not attend. Phillip Newell had to pull up his Teamster dues payments on his phone and show them he was a member.[8]

During the hearing, Ron Schwab, who handled movie duties for the Teamsters, talked about how he had taken over movie production contracts because of Clay's inertia. Other stewards talked about the lack of grievance hearings and any representation from the leadership. Some of the performers were taken aback by Clay's demeanor during the hearing. He winked and smirked at his supporters in the audience. The hearing was interrupted several times by jeering. By the end of the day, the three hundred attendees had dwindled to just a handful, as they still had to work their shifts at the Disney parks and other places.

The panel told the Local 385 members that they would accept written testimony from anyone who was not able to make the hearing or had not been able to speak before them. Phillip Newell and Donnita later mailed them a package of testimonies from Disney workers that weighed several pounds. Even after that, Phillip Newell and Donnita kept up a pressure campaign by sending emails and letters to Hoffa's office.

On the last Monday in June 2019, a notice was posted inside the glass door of the entrance to the Local 385 union hall so that all could read it. Signed by James Hoffa, the notice informed members that the Local 385 was being put into trusteeship and Clay was being removed from his job. When Ralph saw the notice, he was ecstatic. "Enough people complained, and they made a great decision," Ralph said. "Hopefully, they will clean house and not leave anybody from the old regime."

The first reason for the trusteeship, Hoffa said, was the side agreement Clay had signed with Disney over the schedulers. The agreement was negotiated without members' knowledge, and they had not been allowed to vote on it. "Teamsters' members performing character scheduling work were required to either abandon their jobs in order to remain in the union or to accept positions in a nonunion department, with loss of the protections of the Teamsters contract, the financial benefits it provided, and membership in Local 385," Hoffa said. "At the hearing, the local union officers failed to provide a credible explanation of why they had agreed to the MOU [memorandum of understanding], why they failed to inform members of the bargaining unit that the MOU had been negotiated, or why they did not submit the MOU for a membership vote as required by the [Teamsters'] Constitution."

Clay and the other leaders of Local 385 failed to provide Hoffa's representatives with "a credible account of their actions," Hoffa said. He noted that an employer had told his representatives that the Local 385 leaders had refused to schedule negotiating sessions for a new collective bargaining contract, and when the representatives asked for a reason, Clay and his team did not respond.

Hoffa said that hundreds of Teamsters members had voted to leave Local 385 and several hundred more were threatening to leave. He highlighted the fact that almost six hundred character performers and other Disney workers were seeking representation from other locals. Hoffa went on to say that members had complained about not having their grievances processed, that they had been prevented from writing grievances, and that stewards had been prevented from enforcing contracts on the shop floor.

"All of the members in these bargaining units have cited lack of representation as the reason for their dissatisfaction with Local 385 and, in some instances, for wanting to leave the Teamsters," Hoffa said. "Based on the Local's non-responsiveness to my personal representatives, as well as letters from the International Union International Brotherhood of Teamsters soliciting a response to the petitions and complaints we have received, I have concluded that the current leadership is unwilling or unable to modify its behavior and provide better representation to its members."[9]

Clay was out. In his place, Hoffa appointed two representatives to oversee the trusteeship: Michael McElmury and Greg Alden. McElmury had been with the Teamsters, working as an organizer, since 1999. He was at the time living in the western part of the state, in Largo, Florida.

"I urge members who may be dissatisfied with the current representation, and are contemplating leaving the Teamsters, to contact the trustees and explain their problems and concerns," Hoffa concluded. "I assure the Teamsters are fully committed to demonstrating the value of Teamster representation and will immediately attempt to address the outstanding grievances and open collective bargaining. While it's regrettable that circumstances have reached this point, I assure you the International Union is prepared to provide whatever personnel and resources are required to ensure your rights under your collective bargaining agreements and the International Constitutional are protected."

Some of the members bristled at his choice of words over having regrets that it had gotten to this point. They believed Hoffa could have and should have acted sooner. "The characters were the reason," Phillip Newell said. "We represent the brand of the company, and it should be an honor to say, 'Mickey Mouse is a Teamster,' and I believe that is what tipped the scale. We want to have representation. Unions play a big role in balancing corporate greed and helping create fairness for employees. It really is a privilege to have a union. But it's a privilege for them to have us as members." In a later report to the US Department of Labor, Hoffa elaborated on his reasons for the trusteeship, adding that "the current leadership is either unwilling or unable to modify its behavior and provide better representation to its members."[10]

When word spread that the trusteeship notice had been posted to the entrance of the union hall, Donna-Lynne could not help herself—she had to see it with her own eyes. She drove over to the Local 385 union hall. She stayed in her car in the parking lot, where she watched through her car window as a locksmith changed the locks on the doors. She tried to keep her exuberance in check. "I had to drive over to see it. I had to see it before I said anything to anyone," Donna-Lynne said. "It just made me giggle. I'm like, 'Um, yeahhhhh!!' Hoffa in that letter calls them out for not doing their jobs properly. There's a bit of vindication because I did do my job."[11]

Donna-Lynne knew McElmury, the new trustee, from Teamsters' meetings in past years, and she thought he was a "good guy" who would do his best to right the ship. But she worried they would just take out Clay while leaving other members of the leadership in place. Clay did not show up at the office that day.

From what members heard, the other top Local 385 leaders, Walt Howard and Rom Dulskis, were laying the problems at Clay's feet in an effort to keep their jobs. While the new trustees knew the basics of contract negotiations, and they were well-versed in union bylaws, they were unfamiliar with how the character department operated. They did not know any of the stewards, and they did not know any of the negotiating history. They would have to learn quickly if they wanted to keep the characters from leaving. Still, there was relief among the character performers. "It felt like victory," Phillip Newell said. "It felt like justice had been served."

Despite claiming a victory, the character department members of Local 385 were still disappointed that no criminal charges had been filed by the independent investigation team. Workers from the International Brotherhood of Teamsters who came in to help with the trusteeship found a backlog of thousands of grievances. Once the backlog was worked through, elections could be held as a preliminary step toward releasing the local from trusteeship.

Before any of that happened, someone filed a complaint, anonymously, with the US Department of Labor, saying the trusteeship was improper, and the agency launched a separate investigation. The Department of Labor investigation found that Clay had violated the Teamsters' constitution by agreeing with Disney to remove the schedulers from union coverage without presenting the proposal to the local's negotiating committee or allowing members to vote on it.

"During the Department's investigation, the incumbent president of Local 385 stated that currently there is a backlog of approximately 3,000 grievances that are somewhere within the grievance process system," the Department of Labor said in an April 2020 letter closing the case. "The investigation showed that many of the grievances processed by Local 385 were rejected by employers because of Local 385's untimely submission of the grievances. Thus, the International imposed a trusteeship upon Local 385 for an allowable purpose."[12]

16

Pandemic

Less than a year after the International Brotherhood of Teamsters took over Local 385 in a trusteeship, Disney World closed its doors. In March 2020, the rapid spread of the new coronavirus forced "the most magical place on Earth" to go dark for more than three months. For about the first month of the park closures, Disney paid salaries and wages and provided health-care coverage to its seventy-seven thousand furloughed workers. Only a bare-bones crew of around two hundred workers was left behind to take care of maintenance, animals, and the resort's lush vegetation. Further into spring, it was apparent that the parks would be closed for some time. In April 2020, the Service Trades Council Union, representing the resort's largest group of workers, reached an agreement with Disney over how to handle the pandemic. Under the deal, Disney would furlough forty-three thousand members. In exchange, workers would keep their medical, dental, and life insurance benefits for the length of the furlough period, up to a year. Seniority and wage rates remained unchanged. "The union agreement provides stronger protections and benefits for 43,000 union workers at Disney than virtually any other furloughed or laid-off workers in the United States," the Service Trades Council Union said.[1]

No one knew when everyone would return, and like many Floridians in the early days of the pandemic, Disney World workers had trouble applying for unemployment benefits because of the state's aggressively difficult application system. Out-of-work Floridians had their applications disappear on-screen before their eyes, or they got bumped off the online system while filling out their forms.[2] Hew Kowalewski, a Disney World food and beverage trainer, had Disney World paying for his health insurance but still needed money to buy groceries and pay rent. "It's the uncertainty that's the worst," said Kowalewski. "How long can I use my savings to pay my rent and food when I don't know when I'm going back to work?"

As it turned out, Disney World would be closed from March 2020 until July 2020, and not everyone would be brought back, since the number of visitors coming to Orlando had taken a substantial hit from the pandemic. Hotel rooms occupancy was down 60 percent from the previous year, and less than half of the forty-three thousand workers in the Service Trades Council Union were initially called back for the reopening. Disney World, like other Orlando theme parks, had new rules upon reopening. All workers and visitors older than two had to wear masks, and anyone with a 100.4 degrees temperature or higher during a temperature check was not allowed in the resort. The parks were operating with a limited number of visitors, anywhere from one-quarter to one-third of the usual capacity. Social distancing markers on the ground showed where patrons could stand while waiting in lines. Also gone were parades, firework shows, and "meet-and-greet" encounters with the character performers. Disney workers were prohibited from taking photos of visitors with the guests' phones, lest they spread the virus through common touching.[3]

By September 2020, the limits on crowd sizes and other restrictions were putting a financial squeeze on Disney World, and the company announced layoffs for twenty-eight thousand workers at its parks in Florida and California. Two-thirds of the planned layoffs were part-time, hourly workers, but they also involved salaried workers. Josh D'Amaro, the chair of Disney Parks, Experiences and Products, said his management team had cut expenses, suspended projects, and modified operations, but it was not enough given restrictions on the number of people allowed into the parks because of social distancing and other pandemic-related measures. "As heartbreaking as it is to take this action, this is the only feasible action we have in light of the prolonged impact of COVID-19 on our business, including limited capacity due to physical distancing requirements and continued uncertainty regarding the duration of the pandemic," D'Amaro said.[4]

As the largest unionized workers' group, the Service Trades Council Union had the most at stake. At the time of the announcement, more than seventy-seven hundred full-time and more than ninety-one hundred part-time employees were on furlough. Initially, Disney wanted to lay off almost fifty-three hundred of those full-time workers and more than eighty-eight hundred of those part-time workers, but the Service Trades Council Union pushed back. After several days of negotiations, the Service Trades Council Union won a concession that no full-time workers would be part of the permanent layoffs but eighty-eight hundred part-time workers would lose their jobs. The deal allowed that any worker who was laid off would be the first in line when Disney started rehiring, and they would maintain their seniority. Full-time workers whose jobs were not there anymore were given the chance to transfer to other jobs in the resort.

"These are unprecedented times," said Matt Hollis, president of the Service Trades Council Union. "It's unfortunate anytime a worker is laid off and the mass layoffs that Disney is facing are extremely difficult for thousands of cast members."

Actors' Equity Association, meanwhile, was dealing with whether the union's actors and singers could return to Disney World to work. About 780 Equity performers were employed at Disney World before the pandemic, and sixty actors were called back to work when the park reopened in the summer of 2020. But the invitation was rescinded after the Actors' Equity Association made public concerns that actors were not going to get tested for the coronavirus regularly or be allowed to wear masks when they performed. The Actors' Equity Association filed a grievance, saying its members faced retaliation for demanding coronavirus tests.[5]

As the union dispute dragged on, Disney World began repurposing shows so that they did not feature Equity performers. In place of "Beauty and the Beast—Live on Stage" at Disney's Hollywood Studios, there was a six-person musical combo that played songs from Disney movies, as well as those from the Star Wars and the Muppets franchises. "Recently, we've had to make some difficult decisions to reduce our workforce as the business impacts from the COVID-19 pandemic have become more long-lasting than anyone could have predicted," said Bettina Buckley, vice president for live entertainment at Disney World. "Determining which shows can return and when is a complex process."[6]

Many Disney actors and performers thought Equity was being too stringent in their requirements and criticized their union for keeping them from working. Some left the actor's union. "The lack of a big picture being seen is infuriating," Disney actor Adam Graham posted in August 2020. "The Equity stuff is just driving me insane. I'm almost beyond words with it and people sabotaging themselves."

The stalemate was eventually broken when Disney World agreed to have a state-run testing site for workers and the public at its resort. The company said the union's demands had no influence on the decision to open a testing site at Disney World. In mid-September, after returning to Savi's Workshop, where Disney visitors put together hand-built Star Wars light sabers, Graham posted, "I performed a show I love that I haven't performed for in 190 days this morning. It felt good."

Just a few days before that, he wrote, "A huge thought in my mind constantly will be those performers, still to return, who deserve to return. I don't take it lightly that we are the first to return and do so in the name of all those still waiting. Many good friends and some great new friends are still furloughed and hurting, and I promise to do what I can to be safe and set the example that shows we can ALL return. Small steps. Intermission is over soon."

The intermission would last longer than anybody expected. Because of the dangers of having thousands of people in an indoor theater during the first year of the pandemic, Disney laid off 720 actors and singers, amounting to more than 90 percent of its Equity workers. The Actors' Equity Association said the laid-off workers would maintain their right to be recalled for job openings in 2021.

Meanwhile, Disney workers with specialized skills were doing side hustles to make ends meet, courtesy of a Facebook group called "Ear For Each Other." There, actors who played Jedis at the park offered acting lessons, bakers from the resorts' restaurants sold cupcakes and birthday cakes to the public, and workers from the costuming department merchandised face masks and headbands.

At the Teamsters, Phillip Newell believed the characters were getting better representation under the trusteeship, but not all the character performers felt that way. Some character captains believed Rom Dulskis had messed up how the character performers were called back to their jobs when the Disney World parks reopened after the COVID-19 closures. Under an agreement with Disney World, the Teamsters said that the character performers would be called back based on their skills and seniority. But Rom was using a performer's seniority as the only criterion. So, by October 2020, half of the character performers were told they would have to work in other departments of the theme parks, like retail stores and as ride attendants, until more spots opened in the character department. The character captains said Local 385 gave them little information about the decisions. "We kept asking the union, and they wouldn't give us answers," said one character captain. "A lot of us were like, 'Whoa. We don't know what's going on.'"

Because Local 385 was using only seniority as the criterion for getting the performers back into their regular jobs as characters, Disney was forced to retrain many who were put into positions that were new to them. "Technically, the people made to take different jobs were never supposed to lose their positions," said the character captain who switched into a retail merchandising job. "A line was drawn on each position entertainment has—captain, attendant, character performer. There were lines drawn. Rom just drew the lines however he wanted."

The character captains felt, in some ways, that Rom's actions were yet another retaliation against the character performers for getting Local 385 put into trusteeship. But they also felt it was a total lack of understanding of how the character department worked. When upset performers finally were able to reach Rom, which was difficult in itself, he told them they should be grateful that the union had saved their jobs.

"It's so disheartening now that things are slowly picking up. We are seeing the light at the end of the tunnel, but people weren't supposed to lose their performing jobs in the first place," the character captain said. "A lot of people are quitting their jobs and leaving Disney because of how this was handled."

17

A Teamsters Twist

Sean Mason and Ralph Singer were upset that Rom Dulskis and Walt Howard had not been removed from their jobs at Local 385, given they felt that the two officials were a big part of the problems, along with Clay. Mason felt that McElmury, the new trustee, was just paying lip service to cleaning house and righting the tilting ship that was the local.

For the Teamsters Union convention in 2021, Sean and Ralph decided to put together a slate of convention delegates that would run against Walt and Rom and other members of the old regime. Sean and Ralph called their slate Teamsters United The Real Oz, while the old guard called themselves the Teamsters Unite! For Stronger Contracts slate. "They should have cleaned out the whole house there," Sean said. "Rom should have gone. Howard should have gone. They should all have been taken out."[1]

Sean and Ralph's slate lost, but they accused Walt and Rom, once again, of using dirty tricks. They lodged a protest, and a Teamsters elections investigator agreed with them, finding that Howard and a supporter had tried to interfere with the campaign of Sean and his slate. The interference took place like this: Two members of Sean's slate were handing out leaflets to Disney bus drivers in the parking lot at Animal Kingdom in Disney World when a steward allied with Howard began yelling at the bus drivers, telling them not to listen to the members from Sean's slate. The steward told the bus drivers, "my bus drivers and I are for Walt Howard" and snatched a flyer out of a bus driver's hand after one of the members of Sean's slate had handed it to the driver. The investigator with the International Brotherhood of Teamsters' Office of the Election Supervisor concluded that the steward had violated the rights of members to hear campaign information and the rights of Sean's slate to provide it. The investigator also determined that Howard had instructed or encouraged the steward to do that. As a remedy, Local 385 was required to post on all worksite bulletin boards at Animal Kingdom that Howard and his steward had violated election rules and prevented other candidates from engaging with members. "The Election Supervisor will not tolerate violation of the Rules," the election's office post said.[2]

Meanwhile, the trusteeship was being challenged on another front. A close ally of Clay's named Gary Brown sued Local 385 in February 2021, challenging the legitimacy of the trusteeship. Brown said the trusteeship had lasted longer than the usual eighteen months and it was time to hold elections. Brown claimed that the election was being delayed in order to give McElmury, the trustee, a better chance of winning should he run. Many members saw Brown as a pawn for Clay. "The alleged reason for the trusteeship was the dissatisfaction of Local 385 members with the elected leadership, for which the best remedy is to give members the right to vote," the lawsuit said. "No reason exists why the members themselves cannot take charge of their own local union and elect new officers."[3]

At the same time, someone sent an anonymous letter to Hoffa, asking when Local 385 members would be able to elect their own officers. "It has been nineteen months now and we still do not have our Local Union back under the control of democratically elected members of Local 385, why not?" the anonymous letter said.

Local 385, in a response to the lawsuit, had an answer. The local was planning to have an election but in late summer 2021. "The question raised by the current application is not whether the IBT will conduct an election but how soon the election will be held," the local's attorneys said.[4]

Local 385's membership had taken a hit from the pandemic. Before the pandemic, and the shuttering of theme parks and hotels in Orlando, Local 385 had nine thousand members, but they lost three thousand of those members in 2020 as the closures of central Florida's tourism industry dragged on. By late 2020, as many as five thousand members were without their regular jobs.

"Nonetheless, certain segments of the membership are still unemployed, with virtually the entire tradeshow industry shut down, rental car companies operating with minimum staff, and more than half the membership employed by Disney still out of work," the local's lawyers said in their response. "Since the trusteeship was motivated in large part by the dissatisfaction of the Disney employees with the prior administration of Local 385 and those members' threat to decertify the IBT, it was especially important for the election to be held at a time the Disney employees were eligible to participate."

Pushing the election back to later in the year meant that more members who had dropped their membership when they lost their jobs would be back at work and paying their dues again. The Teamster lawyers also said that to encourage more participation, the local had gotten a waiver from the International Brotherhood of Teamsters to open the vote to members who had not regularly paid their monthly dues in the past two years, as previously required. "Hopefully with the improving medical situation, many of these members will be back at work by this summer and will be paying their current dues," Hoffa wrote to McElmury in February 2021.

The Teamster lawyers also said it would be too confusing to have the election of the officers at the same time as elections for delegates to the international convention. They also linked the anonymous letter to the lawsuit. "While the IBT cannot determine the author of the letter demanding an explanation of its plans for the future course of trusteeship, certainly the lack of any identification, including the absence of a return address, strongly suggests that the author had no good faith interest in obtaining information," the Teamster lawyers said. "Rather, it suggests a wholly manufactured effort to provide support for the contention in the instant lawsuit that the mass of members was beseeching the IBT to schedule an election and that the IBT had ignored such pleas, leaving the court as the last option."

McElmury was more direct in tying Brown's lawsuit to Clay. "He opposed the trusteeship and served as the representative of the former principal officer, Clay Jeffries, defending him during the internal union hearings," McElmury said in court papers. "According to both the General President's findings and the DOL investigation, Jeffries was primarily responsible for the breach of some members' rights to ratify collective bargaining agreements establishing their terms and conditions of employment that led to the trusteeship. Gary Brown has never asked about the trusteeship, filed a letter requesting that the trusteeship be terminated, or otherwise complained about the length of the trusteeship prior to filing the instant lawsuit."[5]

An election was finally held in August 2021. Undeterred after losing the delegates election earlier in the year, Ralph, Sean, Steve Davison, and other reformers once again ran on The Real Oz slate. McElmury, the trustee, ran on another team. The third, old guard-dominated slate was led by Walt Howard, Rom Dulskis, and others who had been Clay's associates. Howard's slate won by a large margin, and the costumed character performers were back in the hands of truckers. The winners took a magnanimous tone in a message after their victory. "We will not fail in our promise to do all we can to advance the labor movement in Florida and build stronger contracts for the Members," they posted. "The real work is ahead of us. In order to accomplish these goals, we need to put politics behind us and come together as Teamsters to bring back unity."[6]

And then a typically weird, Teamster-style twist happened. A trustee on the winning slate led by Walt Howard decided to retire. The retirement created a vacancy that set off a runoff election in summer 2022 between the two candidates with the next-highest totals for that position: Sean Mason and Steve Davison from The Real Oz slate. Sean won with 60 percent of the vote. After a half-decade of investigations, a trusteeship, a failed election, and the departures of hundreds of members because of their unhappiness with their union, there was now a reformer in the ranks of the Local 385's leadership. Less than a month into his new role, Sean already was reviewing the financial books and questioning food and mileage expenses incurred by the local's leaders. "I'm sure they're not happy that I'm here," he said.[7]

Conclusion

Unions are expected to be armies, town halls, and businesses, in that they are expected to fight for their members, be open to their members' (sometimes dissonant) voices, and pay their bills on time. "It is rare for a union or its leadership to realize a good balance of these conflicting demands," a group of labor scholars wrote recently.[1] Teamsters Local 385 leaders struggled with that balance and ultimately failed their members as the local moved away from the principles of union democracy and aimed its wrath at the costumed character performers at Walt Disney World in the late 2010s.

Labor scholar George Strauss has argued that union democracy is desirable not only because it's noble or good in itself but because it increases the effectiveness of the union's work on behalf of its members. "The best we can hope for is responsive leadership," Strauss wrote. "But to insure continued responsive leadership requires that members be able to oppose their leaders' policies and to change their leaders if they become irresponsive—and to do this without great personal cost. Thus, a reasonable requirement of democracy is that it allows low-cost opposition."[2]

In Local 385's case, the cost was high. Efforts to reform the leadership cost Donna-Lynne her job. Local 385 leaders alienated a crucial segment of the membership and caused hundreds of members, if not more, to leave the union. The leadership was not responsive to the needs of the local's members, and there was a lack of financial transparency. Ultimately, members required the intervention of James Hoffa, the top leader of the International Brotherhood of Teamsters.

Democracy in unions isn't easy. It can be messy and difficult to sustain. Leaders who become entrenched in their jobs can lose touch with the needs of their rank-and-file members. "They adopt a different style of life and different values," Strauss wrote. "They become increasingly sympathetic to management and increasingly intolerant to 'trouble-making' dissidents."[3]

A union can have elections, a constitution, an investigative arm, and other trappings of democracy like the Teamsters did. But they don't mean much if these elements—which in combination some call a "safety valve," allowing members to change things if they are unhappy—get "sticky" when being utilized, Strauss writes.[4]

What can be done? The case of Local 385 inspires recommendations that can help locals maintain the principals of union democracy among their ranks. Some of the recommendations already are on the books at some unions but they aren't followed in practice.

- Eliminate slates of candidates with similar ideologies or sympathies and allow candidates to run individually. This will provide a mix of viewpoints in the leadership, rather than sycophants of the union head, and provide a check on the local president.

- Add outside members from other locals to a local union's executive board. These will be independent voices with no allegiance to the local's president, and they can make decisions or express opinions without feeling beholden to the leadership team.

- Have a formal appeals process for a local president's decisions or an internal grievance process for members who are unhappy or feel targeted by decisions. The process of asking the Teamsters investigative arm or the International Brotherhood of Teamsters in Washington, DC, to intervene took too long in the case of Local 385 and intervening was solely up to the discretion of the people in those positions.

- Require the maximum financial transparency. Make a refusal by local leaders to open the books to members an offense that can get a local president removed from office.

- Limit the number of years leaders can serve in their positions. As Strauss notes, "becoming a business agent or national office may mean a wholly new standard of living and way of life. Once elected, such officers will fight determinedly to save their jobs, using all means, fair or foul." Term limits would reduce those incentives for leaders to keep their jobs at all costs.[5]

In their paper "Breaking the Iron Law of Oligarchy: Union Revitalization in the American Labor Movement," labor scholars Kim Voss and Rachel Sherman state that a crisis in the leadership of a union local, such as a trusteeship, can lead to its revitalization. But key to a revitalized local are an influx of fresh leadership, a desire to shake up the status quo by mobilizing members, and assistance from the local's international union. "Any one of these factors alone was not enough to spur full revitalization; only in combination do they explain why fully revitalized locals both had staff committed to making changes and were successful in making those changes, while others did not," they wrote.[6] It would seem, then, that Local 385 still is working toward revitalization, as of this writing in early 2023, so that its members can have their fairy-tale ending.

Acknowledgments

To the members of Local 385 who shared their stories with me, thank you.
    I'd also like to thank my partner, Erdem, whose wisdom and good humor are always in abundance.

Notes

Introduction

1 U.S. Bureau of Labor Statistics. Union Members Summary–2021 A01 Results (bls .gov), union-membership-in-the-united-states.pdf (bls.gov).
2 Steven K. Ashby, "Union Democracy in Today's Labor Movement," Labor Studies Journal 2022 47, no. 2 (2021): 109–36, 5.
3 Ashby, "Union Democracy in Today's Labor Movement," 7.

Chapter 1. The Marriage

1 Carl Crosslin, interview by the author, Winter Park, Florida, May 2019 (hereafter the Crosslin interview).
2 Dana Frank, "The Devil and Mr. Hearst," Nation, June 2, 2000.
3 Walt Disney World Co. and Local 855 International Alliance of Theatrical Stage Employees and Motion Picture Machine Operators of the United States and Canada, AFL-CIO, Petitioner. Cases 12-RC-4527 and 12-RC-4531. Decision and Order, December 9, 1974 (hereafter Decision and Order, December 9, 1974).
4 Decision and Order, December 9, 1974.
5 Decision and Order, December 9, 1974.
6 Crosslin interview.
7 Crosslin interview.
8 "Disney World Characters to Join Teamsters' Union," Associated Press, August 20, 1982.
9 Crosslin interview.

Chapter 2. Little Snow White

1 Interview of Donna-Lynne Dalton by the author, Winter Park, Florida, May 2019 (hereafter the Dalton, May 2019 interview).
2 Interview of Donna-Lynne Dalton and her mother, Barbara, by the author, Orlando, Florida, February 22, 2020 (hereafter the Dalton, February 2020 interview).
3 Interview of Donna-Lynne Dalton by the author, Orlando, Florida, May 21, 2015 (hereafter the Dalton, May 2015 interview).
4 Interview of Donna-Lynne Dalton by the author, Orlando, Florida, June 14, 2020 (hereafter the Dalton, June 14, 2020, interview).

Chapter 3. Getting into Character

1 Dalton, May 2015 interview.
2 Interview of Mark Behrens by the author, Orlando, Florida, July 21, 2020 (hereafter the Behrens interview).
3 Josh D'Amaro, April 13, 2021, "A Place Where Everyone Is Welcome," Disney Parks Blog. A Place Where Everyone is Welcome | Disney Parks Blog (go.com)
4 Mike Schneider, "Disney Changing Splash Mountain Ride Tied to Jim Crow Film," *Associated Press,* June 25, 2020.
5 Internal company document, Your Role in the Disney World Show, 1975.
6 Dalton, May 2015 interview.
7 Dalton, May 2015 interview.
8 Interview of Susi Rivera by the author, Orlando, Florida, April 2, 2020 (hereafter the Rivera interview).
9 Behrens interview.
10 Cher Krause Knight, *Power and Paradise in Walt Disney's World* (Gainesville: University Press of Florida, 2014), 158–59.
11 Rivera interview.
12 Rivera interview.
13 Agreement Between Walt Disney Parks and Resorts U.S. and The Service Trades Council Union (Regular Full Time). Effective September 24, 2017 (hereafter Agreement, September 24, 2017).
14 Agreement, September 24, 2017.
15 Mike Schneider, "Tigger Actor Acquitted of Fondling Teen," *Associated Press,* August 4, 2004.
16 Agreement Walt Disney Parks and Resorts U.S. and The Service Trades Council Union (Regular Full Time). Effective March 30, 2014.
17 Mike Schneider, "Disney and Orlando: 30 Years of a Sometimes-Rocky Marriage," *Associated Press,* September 15, 2001.
18 Schneider, "Disney and Orlando."

Chapter 4. The Rat's Nest

1 Interview of Donna-Lynne Dalton, June 23, 2020 (hereafter the Dalton, June 23, 2020, interview).
2 Interview of John "Spike" Coskey, September 13, 2018 (hereafter the Coskey interview).
3 Nelson Lichtenstein, *State of the Union: A Century of American Labor* (Princeton, N.J.: Princeton University Press, 2002), 23–36.
4 James B. Jacobs and Kerry T. Cooperman, *Breaking the Devil's Pact: The Battle to Free the Teamsters from the Mob* (New York: New York University Press, 2011), 11.
5 Dan La Botz, *Rank and File Rebellion* (London: Verso, 1990), 137–38.
6 Ibid.
7 F. C. "Duke" Zeller, *Devil's Pact: Inside the World of the Teamsters Union* (Secaucus, NJ: Birch Lane Press, 1996), 13–16.

8 Committee on Education and the Workforce, Subcommittee on Oversight and Investigations. "Report on the Financial, Operating and Political Affairs of the International Brotherhood of Teamsters," February 24, 1999.
9 Frank Swoboda, "In the District, Chipping Away at the Teamsters' Gilt Edge," *Washington Post*, March 28, 1995.
10 Committee on Education and the Workforce, Subcommittee on Oversight and Investigations, "Report on the Financial, Operating and Political Affairs of the International Brotherhood of Teamsters," February 24, 1999.
11 Zeller, *Devil's Pact*, 30–31.
12 La Botz, *Rank and File Rebellion*, 322.
13 Ryan Patrick Alford and James Jacobs, "The Teamsters Rocky Road to Recovery," *New York University School of Law, Public Law & Legal Theory Research Paper Series*. Working Paper No. 06-22, August 2006.
14 Vicki Vaughan, "Teamsters Convention in Orlando Has All the Makings of a TV Drama," *Orlando Sentinel*, June 1991.
15 Zeller, *Devil's Pact*, 94–95.
16 Lichtenstein, *State of the Union*, 144–46.
17 Teamsters Structure, International Brotherhood of Teamsters.
18 Zeller, *Devil's Pact*, 123.
19 Election Office Case No. P-668-385-SEC.
20 Election Office Case No. P-1147-LU385-SEC.
21 Zeller, *Devil's Pact*, 126–27.
22 Committee on Education and the Workforce report, 18.
23 Zeller, *Devil's Pact*, 179–89.
24 Interview of Sean Mason, October 16, 2018 (hereafter the Mason, 2018 interview).
25 Proposed Charges Concerning Former Local 385 President Larry Parker, from Members of the Independent Review Board, September 12, 1995.
26 United States of America, plaintiff-appellee v. Paul Henry Parker, defendant-appellant, 586 F.2d 422 (5th Circuit 1978).
27 Vicki Vaughan, "Reformers Win Control of Teamsters," *Orlando Sentinel*, January 7, 1994.
28 Vaughan, "Reformers Win Control of Teamsters."
29 International Brotherhood of Teamsters, Local 385 (Freeman Decorating Services, Inc.) and Doris Caraballo, National Labor Relations Board, Division of Judges, "Decision and Order," November 23, 2020.
30 Ashby, "Union Democracy in Today's Labor Movement," 11.
31 Dalton, June 2020 interview.

Chapter 5. All Politics Is Local

1 Coskey interview.
2 Vicki Vaughan, "Protesters Turn Car into Hunk of Junk at Hotel Site," *Orlando Sentinel*, July 16, 1988.
3 Coskey interview.

4 Coskey interview.

5 Ashby, "Union Democracy in Today's Labor Movement," 16.

Chapter 6. Clean Underwear

1 Mike Schneider, "Disney Characters Win Right to Clean Underwear," *Associated Press*, June 7, 2001.

2 Interview of Steve Pollino by the author, Orlando, Florida, July 1, 2019 (hereafter the Pollino interview).

3 Interview with Teresa Freeman by the author, Orlando, Florida, July 1, 2019 (hereafter the Freeman interview).

4 Interview with Donna-Lynne Dalton by the author, Orlando, Florida, June 6, 2018 (hereafter the Dalton, June 2018 interview).

5 Mike Schneider, "Parade Float Kills Disney Worker," *Associated Press*, February 11, 2004.

6 Agreement Between Walt Disney Parks and Resorts U.S. and The Service Trades Council Union (Regular Full Time). Effective September 24, 2017.

7 Internal document, The Disney Look, Disney 2013.

8 Heather Weaver and Gurjot Kaur, personal communication, May 21, 2015.

9 Imane Boudal v. Walt Disney Corporation, "Complaint for Damages," August 10, 2012.

10 Mike Schneider, "Disney Loosens Up Dress Code, Grooming Standards," *Associated Press*, July 12, 2003.

11 D'Amaro blog post.

12 Mike Schneider, "Disney Loosens Up Dress Code, Grooming Standards," *Associated Press*, July 12, 2003.

13 Jonathan VanBoskerck, "I Love Disney World but Wokeness is Ruining the Experience," *Orlando Sentinel*, April 23, 2021.

14 Mike Schneider, "Disney World's Confidentiality Warning Riles Actors' Union," *Associated Press*, June 5, 2015.

15 Pollino interview.

16 Dalton, May 2019 interview.

17 Agreement, September 2017.

18 Arbitration, Opinion and Award in the Matter Between Walt Disney World Company and Teamsters Local 385, April 27, 2015.

19 Agreement, September 2017.

20 Arbitration, Opinion and Award in the Matter Between Walt Disney World Company and Teamsters Local 385. April 27, 2015.

21 "Disney Teamsters Win Wrongful Termination Case," *Press release from International Brotherhood of Teamsters,* April 30, 2015.

Chapter 7. Disney Labor

1 Jim Korkis, *The Unofficial Walt Disney World 1971 Companion: Stories of How the World Began* (Orlando: Theme Park Press, 2019), 23.

2 Korkis, *The Unofficial Walt Disney World 1971 Companion*, 20–22.

3 Mark Andrews, "Disney Assembled Cast of Buyers to Amass Land Stage for Kingdom," *Orlando Sentinel,* May 30, 1993.

4 Emily Bavar, "Is Our 'Mystery' Industry Disneyland?" *Orlando Sentinel,* October 21, 1965.

5 Kenneth Michael, "Echoing Unions' Struggle," *Orlando Sentinel,* August 27, 1989.

6 "Disney Starts Contract Talks," *Orlando Sentinel,* May 28, 1968.

7 Korkis, *The Unofficial Walt Disney World 1971 Companion,* 97–98.

8 "Help Wanted But Only Pretty Girls with Happy, Friendly Spirits," *Orlando Sentinel,* February 28, 1971.

9 "VIP Posts at Walt Disney World Prepared For World Leader Visits," *Walt Disney World news release,* 1971.

10 Internal company document, *A Guide for Walt Disney World Representatives,* 1969.

11 Donn Tatum letter, undated.

12 Undated internal document, *Courtesy Reminders.*

13 Interview of George Kalogridis, August 30, 2021 (hereafter Kalogridis interview).

14 Interview of Forrest Bahruth, August 30, 2021 (hereafter the Bahruth interview).

15 Interview of Barbara Maxwell, August 30, 2021 (hereafter the Maxwell interview).

16 Interview of Chuck Milam, August 31, 2021 (hereafter Milam interview).

17 Kalogridis interview.

18 Reedy Creek Improvement District Comprehensive Plan 2020, October 7, 2010.

19 Mike Schneider, "Union Faces Tough Negotiations as Belt-Tightening Comes to Disney World," *Associated Press,* April 16, 2001.

20 Lee Cockerell, *Creating Magic: 10 Common Sense Leadership Strategies from a Life at Disney* (New York: Currency, 2008), 5.

21 International Alliance of Theatrical Stage Employees and Moving Picture Machine Operators of the United States and Canada and Walt Disney World Co., Case 12-CB-1429. Decision and Order, December 5, 1974.

22 Mike Schneider, "Vote at Universal Seen as Bellwether for Unions' Chances in Orlando," *Associated Press,* April 18, 1999.

23 John Wark and Kathryn Phillips, "Epcot Workers Walk Out," *Orlando Sentinel Star,* October 1980.

24 "Striking Disney World Musicians Return to Work Under New Contract," *Orlando Sentinel Star,* October 28, 1980.

25 Mike Schneider, "Workers at Disney World's Dolphin and Swan hotels go on strike," *Associated Press,* May 28, 2002.

26 Gabriel San Roman, "How the Disneyland Strike of 1984 Changed the Magic Kingdom Forever," *OC Weekly,* March 23, 2018.

27 Internal company document, *Destination . . . Walt Disney World,* 1973.

28 Gabriel San Roman, "How the Disneyland Strike of 1984 Changed the Magic Kingdom Forever," *OC Weekly,* March 23, 2018.

29 Vicki Vaughan, "Union Talks with Disney at Impasse," *Orlando Sentinel,* October 30, 1985.

30 Vicki Vaughan, "Disney Unions Focus on Wages," *Orlando Sentinel,* September 23, 1987.

31 Kim Moody, *An Injury to All: The Decline of American Unionism* (London: Verso, 1988), 2–5.
32 Vicki Vaughan, "Cheating Lets the Air out of Disney Vote," *Orlando Sentinel*, November 12, 1998.
33 Adam Yeomans, "Wages Are Sore Point at Disney," *Orlando Sentinel*, November 16, 1988.
34 Vicki Vaughan, "Disney Enters Tense New Era with Workers," *Orlando Sentinel*, November 20, 1988.
35 Moody, *An Injury to All*, 303.
36 Cockerell, *Creating Magic*, 62.
37 Walt Disney World Co. and Actor's Equity Association, Case 12-CA-18484, Decision and Order, October 26, 1999.
38 Sandra Pedicini, "Disney Will Pay $3.8 million in Back Wages after Feds Allege Wage and Hour Violations," *Orlando Sentinel*, March 17, 2017.

Chapter 8. Fifteen Dollars an Hour or Bust

1 Interview of Ed Chambers, March 23, 2018 (hereafter the Chambers, March 2018 interview).
2 Chabeli Carrazana, "In a Theme Park Parking Lot at Night, a Worker Sleeps in Her Car. This Is Life in America's Most Visited City," *Orlando Sentinel*, December 5, 2019.
3 Chambers, March 2018 interview.
4 Jake Rosenfeld, *What Unions No Longer Do* (Cambridge, Mass.: Harvard University Press, 2014), 92–99.
5 Chambers, March 2018 interview.
6 Kerri Anne Renzulli, "Disney Isn't the Only Company Paying Its CEO 1,000 Times More Than Its Typical Employee Earns: Here Are 12 Others," *CNBC.com*, April 23, 2019.
7 Interview of Donna-Lynne Dalton, December 5, 2017 (hereafter the Dalton, December 2017 interview).

Chapter 9. Unhappiness

1 Regular Called Executive Board Meeting Held on July 15, 2016.
2 Interview of Steve Davison, December 4, 2018 (hereafter the Davison interview).
3 International Brotherhood of Teamsters v. Hector L. Santana-Quintana, National Labor Relations Board, Division of Judges, "Decision," March 22, 2017.
4 Ashby, "Union Democracy in Today's Labor Movement," 26.
5 Lichtenstein, *State of the Union*, 142.
6 Lichtenstein, *State of the Union*, 142.
7 Jamie Peck, "The Right to Work, and the Right at Work," *Economic Geography*, January 2016.
8 Phillip B. Wilson, "Avoidance: 5 Keys to Winning Your Union Election," *LRI Management Services*, 2016.

9 Celine McNicholas, "Unlawful: U.S. Employers Are Charged with Violating Federal Law in 41.5% of All Union Election Campaigns," *Economic Policy Institute,* December 11, 2019.

10 Coskey interview.

11 International Brotherhood of Teamsters v. Hector L. Santana-Quintana, National Labor Relations Board, Division of Judges, "Decision," March 22, 2017.

12 Coskey interview.

13 Interview of Sean Mason, December 2017 (hereafter the Mason, 2017 interview).

14 Interview of Ralph Singer, December 4, 2018 (hereafter the Singer, December 2018 interview).

15 Ashby, "Union Democracy in Today's Labor Movement," 11.

16 Ashby, "Union Democracy in Today's Labor Movement," 11.

17 Form LM-2 Labor Organization Annual Report.

18 Singer, December 2018 interview.

19 Ashby, "Union Democracy in Today's Labor Movement," 14.

20 Ashby, "Union Democracy in Today's Labor Movement," 15.

21 Singer, 2018 interview.

22 Mason, 2017 interview.

23 Davison interview.

24 U.S. Department of Labor, Office of Labor-Management Standards, May 9, 2016, letter to Michael Stapleton on audit.

25 Dalton, December 2017 interview.

26 United States of America v. International Brotherhood of Teamsters, "Declaration in Support of the Independent Investigations Officer's Application for the Issuance of a Subpoena Directing Regions Bank to Produce Specified Records," Exhibits 1–7, November 20, 2017.

27 Dalton, December 2017 interview.

Chapter 10. Election

1 Pollino interview.

2 Interview of Jonathan Sidwell by the author, Orlando, Florida, July 1, 2019 (hereafter the Sidwell interview).

3 Interview of John Dodson by the author, Orlando, Florida, July 1, 2019 (hereafter the Dodson interview).

4 Dalton, December 2017 interview.

5 Ashby, "Union Democracy in Today's Labor Movement," 16.

6 Dalton, December 2017 interview.

7 Singer, December 2018 interview.

8 George Strauss, "Union Democracy," *UC-Berkeley Working Paper Series,* February 25, 1991.

Chapter 11. Retaliation

1 Dalton, December 2017 interview.

2 Singer, December 2018 interview.

3 Davison interview.
4 State of Florida v. Roger Allain, filed May 22, 2019.
5 James Hoffa memo to Local 385, February 28, 2019.
6 Davison interview.
7 Sidwell interview.
8 Freeman interview.
9 Members First, Facebook, December 3, 2017.
10 Gabrielle Russon, "Union Workers Reject Disney's Wage Proposal," *Orlando Sentinel*, December 20, 2017.

Chapter 12. Mickey Mouse Revolts

1 Walt Disney World characters petition.
2 Interview of Donna-Lynne Dalton by the author, Orlando, Florida, January 18, 2018 (hereafter the Dalton, January 2018 interview).
3 Interview of Joe Maseda by the author, Orlando, Florida, January 26, 2018 (hereafter the Maseda interview).
4 Interview of Donnita Coleman-DuBell by the author, Orlando, Florida, January 19, 2018 (hereafter the Coleman-DuBell interview).
5 Singer, December 2018 interview.

Chapter 13. Contract

1 Interview of Ed Chambers, May 1, 2018 (hereafter the Chambers, May 2018 interview).
2 Mike Schneider, "Disney Workers Approve New Contract Raising Minimum Wage," *Associated Press*, September 6, 2018.
3 Interview of Phillip Newell, June 25, 2019 (hereafter the Newell interview).

Chapter 14. Leaving

1 Interview of Donna-Lynne Dalton, January 23, 2019 (hereafter the Dalton, January 2019 interview).

Chapter 15. A Reckoning

1 International Brotherhood of Teamsters notice from James P. Hoffa, June 24, 2019.
2 Memorandum of Understanding 2017 Walt Disney Parks and Resorts U.S. and the International Brotherhood of Teamsters Local 385, "Scheduling Duties," September 14, 2018.
3 Mason, 2018 interview.
4 Dodson interview.
5 Interview of Donna-Lynne Dalton, April 13, 2019 (hereafter the Dalton, April 2019 interview).
6 United States Government National Labor Relations Board, Dismissal of Appeal, Case 12-CA-234520, August 12, 2019.

7 James Hoffa memo to Local 385, February 28, 2019.

8 Newell interview.

9 International Brotherhood of Teamsters notice from James P. Hoffa, June 24, 2019.

10 Form LM-15 Trusteeship Report for Teamsters Local 385, U.S. Department of Labor, Office of Labor-Management Standards, July 29, 2019.

11 Interview of Donna-Lynne Dalton in Orlando, Florida, June 25, 2019 (hereafter the Dalton, June 2019 interview).

12 U.S. Department of Labor, Office of Labor-Management Standards, Division of Enforcement, *Statement of Reasons for Dismissing a Complaint Alleging the Improper Imposition of a Trusteeship on Local 385 by the International Brotherhood of Teamsters,* April 7, 2020.

Chapter 16. Pandemic

1 Mike Schneider, "Disney World Furloughing 43,000 More Workers Due to Virus," *Associated Press,* April 11, 2020.

2 Mike Schneider, "Disney World Workers Take Aim at Florida's Jobless System," *Associated Press,* April 13, 2020.

3 Mike Schneider, "Workers Praise Disney Virus Safety But Will Visitors Come?" *Associated Press,* July 26, 2020.

4 Mike Schneider, "Disney to Lay Off 28,000 at Its Parks in California, Florida," *Associated Press,* September 29, 2020.

5 Mike Schneider, "Actors and Disney World Reach Deal after Virus Testing Fight," *Associated Press,* August 12, 2020.

6 Bettina Buckley, "Update on Entertainment at Walt Disney World Resort," *Disney Parks Blog,* October 30, 2020.

Chapter 17. A Teamsters Twist

1 Interview of Sean Mason by author in Orlando, Florida, March 25, 2021 (hereafter the Mason, March 2021 interview).

2 Office of the Election Supervisor for the International Brotherhood of Teamsters in re: Cody Johnson. Protest Decision 2021 ESD 74.

3 Gary Brown v. International Brotherhood of Teamsters, "Complaint," February 22, 2021.

4 Gary Brown v. International Brotherhood of Teamsters, "Answer of International Brotherhood of Teamsters," March 23, 2021.

5 Gary Brown v. International Brotherhood of Teamsters, "Memorandum of International Brotherhood of Teamsters in Opposition to Motion for Preliminary Injunction," April 2, 2021.

6 Teamsters United for Stronger Contracts Slate, Teamsters UNITE for Stronger Contracts Slate | Facebook.

7 Interview of Sean Mason, July 30, 2022 (hereafter the Mason, 2022 interview).

Conclusion

1 Margaret Levi, David Olson, Jon Agnone, and Devin Kelly, "Union Democracy Reexamined," *Politics & Society* 37, no. 2 (June 2009): 203–28.

2 Strauss, "Union Democracy," 1.

3 Strauss, "Union Democracy," 4–5.

4 Strauss, "Union Democracy," 4–5.

5 Strauss, "Union Democracy," 20.

6 Kim Voss and Rachel Sherman, "Breaking the Iron Law of Oligarchy: Union Revitalization in the American Labor Movement," *American Journal of Sociology* 06, no. 2 (September 2000): 303–49.

Bibliography

ACLU/The Sikh Coalition letter. May 21, 2015.

Actors' Equity Association. "Agreement and Rules Governing Employment at Walt Disney World." September 21, 2008.

Agreement Between Walt Disney Parks and Resorts U.S. and The Service Trades Council Union (Regular Full Time). Effective March 30, 2014.

Agreement Between Walt Disney World and North America's Building and Trades Unions and Craft Maintenance Council. October 2, 2016.

Agreement Between Walt Disney Parks and Resorts U.S. and The Service Trades Council Union (Regular Full Time). Effective September 24, 2017.

Alcorn, Steve, and David Green. *Building a Better Mouse: The Story of the Electronic Imagineers Who Designed EPCOT*. Orlando, Fla.: Theme Perks Press, 2007.

Alford, Ryan Patrick, and James Jacobs. "The Teamsters Rocky Road to Recovery." New York University School of Law. *Public Law & Legal Theory Research Paper Series. Working Paper No. 06–22*. August 2006.

Andrews, Mark. "Disney Assembled Cast of Buyers to Amass Land Stage for Kingdom." *Orlando Sentinel*, May 30, 1993.

Arbitration Opinion and Award Before Robert B. Moberly, Arbitrator. In the Matter Between Walt Disney World and Teamster Local 385. April 27, 2015.

Ashby, Steven K. "Union Democracy in Today's Labor Movement." *Labor Studies Journal 2022* 47, no. 2: 109–36.

Bavar, Emily. "Is Our 'Mystery' Industry Disneyland?" *Orlando Sentinel*, October 21, 1965.

Brill, Steven. *The Teamsters*. New York: Simon & Schuster, 1978.

Buckley, Bettina. "Update on Entertainment at Walt Disney World Resort." *Disney Parks Blog*, October 30, 2020.

Carlson, Peter. "Teamster Glasnost." *Washington Post*, December 8, 1991.

Carranza, Chabeli. "In a Theme Park Parking Lot at Night, Worker Sleeps in Her Car. This is Life in America's Most Visited City." *Orlando Sentinel*, December 5, 2019.

Cockerell, Lee. *Creating Magic: 10 Common Sense Leadership Strategies from a Life at Disney*. New York: Currency, 2008.

Committee on Education and the Workforce, Subcommittee on Oversight and Investigations. "Report on the Financial, Operating and Political Affairs of the International Brotherhood of Teamsters." February 24, 1999.

Cullen, Bonnie. "For Whom the Shoe Fits: Cinderella in the Hands of Victorian Writers and Illustrators." Project Muse. *The Lion and the Unicorn* 27, no. 1 (January 2003): 57–82.

Dreier, Peter, and Daniel Fleming. "Working for the Mouse: A Survey of Disneyland Resort Employees." Occidental College Urban & Environmental Policy Institute and the Economic Roundtable, 2018.

"Disney Reaches Agreement on Pay Practices with US Department of Labor." *News Release from the U.S. Department of Labor.* March 17, 2017.

"Disney World Characters to Join Teamsters' Union." *Associated Press,* August 20, 1982.

"Division Announces Staff Additions; Welcomes Disney, Amusement Parks to the Fold." *International Brotherhood of Teamsters Announcement.* April 22, 2022.

Election Office Case Numbers P-929-LU385-SEC and P-35-LU385-SEC. Office of the Election Officer c/o International Brotherhood of Teamsters. October 10, 1991.

Election Office Case Number P-668-385-SEC. April 18, 1996.

Election Office Case Number P-1147-LU385-SEC. November 18, 1996.

Election Office Case Number PR-043-LU385-SCE. January 9, 1998.

Election Office Case Number PR-060-LU385-SEC. May 12, 1998.

Foglesong, Richard E. *Married to the Mouse: Walt Disney World and Orlando.* New Haven, Conn.: Yale University Press, 2001.

Form LM-2 Labor Organization Annual Report for Teamsters Local 385, U.S. Department of Labor, Office of Labor-Management Standards, January 1, 2019, to December 31, 2019.

Form LM-2 Labor Organization Annual Report for Teamsters Local 385, U.S. Department of Labor, Office of Labor-Management Standards, January 1, 2018, to December 31, 2018.

Form LM-15 Trusteeship Report for Teamsters Local 385, U.S. Department of Labor, Office of Labor-Management Standards, July 29, 2019.

Form LM-15 Trusteeship Report for Teamsters Local 385, U.S. Department of Labor, Office of Labor-Management Standards, March 11, 2020.

Form LM-15 Trusteeship Report for Teamsters Local 385, U.S. Department of Labor, Office of Labor-Management Standards, August 17, 2020.

Frank, Dana. "The Devil and Mr. Hearst." *Nation,* June 2, 2000.

Friedman, Jake S. *The Disney Revolt: The Great Labor War of Animation's Golden Age.* Chicago: Chicago Review Press, 2022.

Gary Brown v. International Brotherhood of Teamsters. "Complaint." February 22, 2021.

Gary Brown v. International Brotherhood of Teamsters. "Plaintiff's Memorandum of Law in Support of His Motion for Preliminary Injunction." February 22, 2021.

Gary Brown v. International Brotherhood of Teamsters. "Answer of International Brotherhood of Teamsters." March 23, 2021.

Gary Brown v. International Brotherhood of Teamsters. "Memorandum of International Brotherhood of Teamsters in Opposition to Motion for Preliminary Injunction." April 2, 2021.

Gary Brown v. International Brotherhood of Teamsters. "Defendant's Report on Status of Trusteeship." September 1, 2021.

Goldfield, Michael. *The Decline of Organized Labor in the United States.* Chicago: University of Chicago Press, 1987.

Greenhouse, Steven. "Workers at 2 Hotels End Strike." *New York Times,* June 11, 2002.

"Help Wanted But Only Pretty Girls With Happy, Friendly Spirits." *Orlando Sentinel,* February 28, 1971.

Imane Boudal v. Walt Disney Corporation. "Complaint for Damages." August 10, 2012.

International Alliance of Theatrical Stage Employees and Moving Picture Machine Operators of the United States and Canada and Walt Disney World Co., Case 12-CB-1429. Decision and Order, December 5, 1974.

International Brotherhood of Teamsters Audit Report. April 26, 2017.

"Disney Teamsters Win Wrongful Termination Case." *International Brotherhood of Teamsters Newsletter.* April 30, 2015.

International Brotherhood of Teamsters notice from James P. Hoffa, June 24, 2019.

International Brotherhood of Teamsters, Local 385 (Freeman Decorating Services, Inc.) and Doris Caraballo. National Labor Relations Board, Division of Judges, "Decision and Order," November 23, 2020.

International Brotherhood of Teamsters v. Hector L. Santana-Quintana, National Labor Relations Board, Division of Judges, "Decision," March 22, 2017.

International Brotherhood of Teamsters v. Hector L. Santana-Quintana, National Labor Relations Board, Division of Judges, "Decision and Order," June 20, 2018.

Jacobs, James B., and Kerry T. Cooperman. *Breaking the Devil's Pact: The Battle to Free the Teamsters from the Mob.* New York: New York University Press, 2011.

James Hoffa memo to Local 385. February 28, 2019.

Kelly, Kim. *Fight Like Hell: The Untold History of American Labor.* New York: Altria, 2022.

Knight, Cher Krause. *Power and Paradise in Walt Disney's World.* Gainesville: University Press of Florida, 2014.

Korkis, Jim. *The Unofficial Walt Disney World 1971 Companion: Stories of How the World Began.* Orlando: Theme Park Press, 2019.

La Botz, Dan. *Rank and File Rebellion.* London: Verso, 1990.

Levi, Margaret, David Olson, Jon Agnone, and Devin Kelly. "Union Democracy Reexamined." *Politics & Society* 37, no. 2 (June 2009): 203–28.

Lichtenstein, Nelson. *State of the Union: A Century of American Labor.* Princeton, N.J.: Princeton University Press, 2002.

Local 385-The Real Oz Slate/Members First Slate. Home. Facebook. December 3, 2017, from (2) Local 385, The Real Oz Slate. Facebook.

McNicholas, Celine. "Unlawful: U.S. Employers are Charged with Violating Law in 41.5% of All Union Election Campaigns." *Economic Policy Institute,* December 11, 2019.

Memorandum of Understanding 2017 Walt Disney Parks and Resorts U.S. and the International Brotherhood of Teamsters Local 385. "Scheduling Duties." September 14, 2018.

McShane Wulfhart, Nell. *The Great Stewardess Rebellion.* New York: Doubleday, 2022.

Michael, Kenneth. "Echoing Unions' Struggle." *Orlando Sentinel,* August 27, 1989.

Moody, Kim. *An Injury to All: The Decline of American Unionism.* London: Verso, 1988.

Peck, Jamie. "The Right to Work, and the Right at Work." *Economic Geography,* January 2016.

Pedicini, Sandra. "Disney Will Pay $3.8 Million in Back Wages After Feds Allege Wage and Hours Violations." *Orlando Sentinel,* March 17, 2017.

Proposed Charges Concerning Former Local 385 President Larry Parker. From Members of the Independent Review Board. September 12, 1995.

"Recall for Character Cast," Memorandum of Understanding. Walt Disney Parks and Resorts U.S. and International Brotherhood of Teamsters Local 385. May 7, 2021.

Reedy Creek Improvement District Comprehensive Plan 2020. October 7, 2010.

Regular Called Executive Board Meeting Held on July 15, 2016.

Renzulli, Kerri Anne. "Disney Isn't the Only Company Paying Its CEO 1,000 Times More Than Its Typical Employee Earns: Here Are 12 Others." *CNBC.com,* April 23, 2019.

Rosenfeld, Jake. *What Unions No Longer Do.* Cambridge, Mass.: Harvard University Press, 2014.

San Roman, Gabriel. "How the Disneyland Strike of 1984 Changed the Magic Kingdom Forever." *OC Weekly,* March 23, 2018.

Russon, Gabrielle. "Union Workers Reject Disney's Wage Proposal." *Orlando Sentinel,* December 20, 2017.

Schneider, Mike. "Disney Characters Win Right to Clean Underwear." *Associated Press,* June 7, 2001.

———. "Disney and Orlando: 30 Years of a Sometimes-Rocky Marriage." *Associated Press,* September 15, 2001.

———. "Workers at Disney World's Dolphin and Swan Hotels Go on Strike." *Associated Press,* May 28, 2002.

———. "Disney Loosens Up Dress Code, Grooming Standards." *Associated Press,* July 12, 2003.

———. "Tigger Actor Acquitted of Fondling Teen." Associated Press, August 4, 2004.

———. "Disney Will Allow Park Workers to Have Beards." *Associated Press,* January 24, 2012.

———. "Disney Told to Rehire Workers Who Refused Soiled Costumes." *Associated Press,* April 28, 2015.

———. "Disney World's Confidentiality Warning Riles Actors' Union." *Associated Press,* June 5, 2015.

———. "Union Faces Tough Negotiations as Belt-Tightening Comes to Disney World." *Associated Press,* April 16, 2001.

———. "Union in Strife as Disney and Teamsters Prepare for Talks." *Associated Press,* August 26, 2017.

———. "Vote at Universal Seen as Bellwether for Unions' Chances." *Associated Press,* April 18, 1999.

———. "Disney Workers Approve New Contract Raising Minimum Wage." *Associated Press,* September 7, 2018.

———. "Disney World Furloughing 43,000 More Workers Due to Virus." *Associated Press,* April 11, 2020.

———. "Disney World Workers Take Aim at Florida's Jobless System." *Associated Press,* April 13, 2020.

———. "Workers Praise Disney Virus Safety But Will Visitors Come?" *Associated Press,* July 26, 2020.

———. "Actors and Disney Reach Deal After Virus Testing Fight." Associated Press, August 12, 2020.

———. "Disney to Lay off 28,000 at Its Parks in California, Florida," *Associated Press,* September 29, 2020.

"Statement of Reasons for Dismissing a Complaint Alleging the Improper Imposition of a Trusteeship on Local 385 by the International Brotherhood of Teamsters." U.S. Department of Labor, Office of Labor-Management Standards, Division of Enforcement, April 7, 2020.

Snow, Richard. *Disney's Land: Walt Disney and the Invention of the Amusement Park That Changed the World.* New York: Scribner, 2019.

Stier, Anderson & Malone, LLC. *The Teamsters: Perception and Reality: Appendix 1, Background Materials.* Washington, D.C.: International Brotherhood of Teamsters, 2002.

Strauss, George. "Union Democracy." *UC-Berkeley Working Paper Series.* February 25, 1991.

"Striking Disney Musicians Return to Work Under New Contract." *Orlando Sentinel Star,* October 28, 1980.

"Teamsters Mark End of Final Order Transition Period." *International Brotherhood of Teamsters News Release.* February 8, 2020.

Swoboda, Frank. "In the District, Chipping Away at the Teamsters' Gilt Edge." *Washington Post,* March 28, 1995.

Teamsters UNITED for Stronger Contracts Slate. Teamsters United 385 Facebook page. (1) Teamsters UNITE for Stronger Contracts Slate. Facebook.

"The Disney Look." Internal company document. Disney. 2013.

"Disney and Service Trades Council Union Settle Tentative Agreement Covering 21,000 Full-Time Cast Members." *United Here Local 737/United Here Local 362 News Release,* July 18, 2014.

United States of America National Labor Relations Board Charge Against Employer, Walt Disney World Co. June 5, 2015.

United States of America National Labor Relations Board Charge Against Employer, International Brotherhood of Teamsters, Local 385, September 1, 2017.

United States of America Before the National Labor Relations Board, Region 12. Walt Disney Parks and Resorts U.S. v. International Brotherhood of Teamsters, Local 385, May 8, 2018.

United States of America v. International Brotherhood of Teamsters. "Notice of Joint Motion for Approval of the Final Agreement and Order and Stipulation of Dismissal." January 13, 2015.

United States of America v. International Brotherhood of Teamsters. "Memorandum of Law in Support of the Independent Investigations Officer's Application for the Issuance of a Subpoena Directing Regions Bank to Produce Specified Records." November 20, 2017.

United States of America v. International Brotherhood of Teamsters. "Declaration in Support of the Independent Investigations Officer's Application for the Issuance of a Subpoena Directing Regions Bank to Produce Specified Records." Exhibits 1–7, November 20, 2017.

United States of America v. International Brotherhood of Teamsters. "Independent Investigations Officer's Application for the Issuance of a Subpoena Directing Regions Bank to Produce Specified Records." November 20, 2017.

United States of America, plaintiff-appellee v. Paul Henry Parker, defendant-appellant. 586 F.2d 422 (5th Circuit 1978).

United States of America National Labor Relations Board. Appeal. Case 12-CB-149949. August 28, 2015.

United States Government National Labor Relations Board. Charge. Teamsters Local 385 (Walt Disney World). Case 12-CB-149937. April 13, 2015.

United States Government National Labor Relations Board. Charge. Teamsters Local 385. Case 12-CA-205576. September 1, 2017.

United States Government National Labor Relations Board. Dismissal of Appeal, Case 12-CA-234520. August 12, 2019.

U.S. Department of Labor, Office of Labor-Management Standards (May 9, 2016). Letter to Michael Stapleton on audit.

U.S. Department of Labor, Office of Labor-Management Standards (November 1, 2018). Letter to Clayton Jeffries.

VanBoskerck, Jonathan. "I Love Disney World, but Wokeness is Ruining the Experience. Commentary." *Orlando Sentinel,* April 23, 2021.

Vaughan, Vicki. "Protesters Turn Car into Hunk of Junk at Hotel Site." *Orlando Sentinel,* July 16, 1988.

———. "Teamsters Convention in Orlando Has All the Makings of a TV Drama." *Orlando Sentinel,* June 1991.

———. "Reformers Win Control of Teamsters." *Orlando Sentinel,* January 7, 1994.

———. "Union Talks with Disney at Impasse." *Orlando Sentinel,* October 30, 1985.

———. "Disney Unions Focus on Wages." *Orlando Sentinel,* September 23, 1987.

———. "Cheating Lets the Air Out of Disney Vote." *Orlando Sentinel,* November 12, 1998.

———. "Disney Enters Tense New Era With Workers." *Orlando Sentinel,* November 20, 1988.

Voss, Kim, and Rachel Sherman. "Breaking the Iron Law of Oligarchy: Union Revitalization in the American Labor Movement." *American Journal of Sociology* 106, no. 2 (September 2000): 303–49.

Walt Disney World Characters petition.

Walt Disney World Co. and Actor's Equity Association. Case 12-CA-18484. Decision and Order, October 26, 1999.

Walt Disney World Co. and Harry E. Winkler and Henry W. Davis. Cases 12-CA-6396 and 12-CA-6396-2. Decision and Order, March 4, 1975.

Walt Disney World Co. and Local 855 International Alliance of Theatrical Stage Employees and Motion Picture Machine Operators of the United States and Canada, AFL-CIO, Petitioner. Cases 12-RC-4527 and 12-RC-4531. Decision and Order, December 9, 1974.

Wark, John, and Kathryn Phillips. "Epcot Workers Walk Out." *Orlando Sentinel Star,* October 1980.

Wilson, Phillip B. "Union Avoidance: 5 Keys to Winning Your Union Election." LRI Management Services, 2016.

Zeller, F. C. "Duke." *Devil's Pact: Inside the World of the Teamsters Union.* Secaucus, N.J.: Birch Lane Press, 1996.

2017 STCU Negotiations. Company Proposal. August 24, 2018.

Yeomans, Adam. "Wages Are Sore Point at Disney." *Orlando Sentinel,* November 16, 1988.

Index

Mike Schneider has been an Associated Press journalist for almost three decades. He has lived in Orlando, Florida, since 1997, reporting on Walt Disney World and the tourism industry, the trials of Casey Anthony and George Zimmerman, the Pulse nightclub massacre and countless hurricanes and space shuttle launches. The St. Louis native has a background in data mapping and covers demographics and the US Census Bureau for AP. He is a graduate of the University of Wisconsin–Madison and the University of Pennsylvania in Philadelphia.